crazy for crab

EVERYTHING YOU NEED TO KNOW

TO ENJOY FABULOUS CRAB AT HOME

Fred Thompson

THE HARVARD COMMON PRESS

BOSTON, MASSACHUSETTS

The Harvard Common Press
535 Albany Street
Boston, Massachusetts 02118
www.harvardcommonpress.com

Printed in England

Library of Congress Cataloging-in-Publication Data
Thompson, Fred.
  Crazy for crab : everything you need to know to enjoy fabulous crab at
home / Fred Thompson.
     p. cm.
  ISBN 1-55832-265-5 (hc) -- ISBN 1-55832-266-3 (pb)
 1. Cookery (Crabs) I. Title.
  TX754.C83.T48 2004
  641.6'95--dc22   2003018903

Special bulk-order discounts are available on this and other Harvard
Common Press books. Companies and organizations may purchase books
for premiums or resale, or may arrange a custom edition, by contacting
the Marketing Director at the address above.

10 9 8 7 6 5 4 3 2 1

Cover and interior design by Barbara Balch
Recipe photography by Brian Hagiwara
Illustrations by Chris Van Dusen
For additional photo credits, see page 200

contents

DEDICATION

For Lil'Bit, you make me proud

acknowledgments

Before I can thank anyone for the help and inspiration I was given on this book, a huge heartfelt thank-you must go to all the men, women, and children who fish the waters of this great country and provide us not only with crabs, but with all the other tasty wonders of the water. It's hard and thankless work, and the people who do it, do it out of pure love of their community, their heritage, and nature. We all need to take a moment and remember these people who hold the keys to the wealth of the feast we put on our tables.

If ever an editor was inspired by a meal, it was Pam Hoenig and her delight over a freshly steamed crab. She was beside me and behind me every step of the way in creating this book. My agent, Lisa Ekus, helped make this book a reality. I'll be forever indebted to a dapper Southern lawyer from Hickory, North Carolina, Young Smith, who 5 years ago put in my hands William Warner's Pulitzer Prize–winning book *Beautiful Swimmers,* and set me on the right path.

So many people in the food world and coastal communities of this land have been kind and giving of their time: Beth Thomas, educational coordinator at the University of South Carolina's Baruch Marine Field Biology Laboratory at Hobcaw Barony, just north of Georgetown, South Carolina, who impressed upon me the absolute necessity of maintaining our saltwater estuaries if we wanted to keep eating seafood; the folks at the Chesapeake Bay Maritime Museum in St. Michaels, Maryland, who pointed me in so many great directions while I was on the Chesapeake Bay; the good people of Crisfield, Maryland, self-proclaimed Crab Capital of the World, who took me in as one of their own; the Crisfield Chamber of Commerce, for some award-winning Crab Derby Days recipes; Heidi Cusick, with the Mendocino (California) County Alliance, who gave so much of herself and her time and introduced me to Dungeness crab country. How can I forget Gene Mattiuzzo, who led me through the processing of Dungeness crab and regaled me with stories about crabbing on the north coast, keeping me laughing the whole time (and not many book interviews end with a toast of 40-year-old moonshine). Thanks to Linda Johnson, who ate all my leftovers and picked crabs when I got tired; Diane Collins, my physical therapist in New York, who became a gung ho crab recipe taster; B. A. and Sam Schlegel, who were a wealth of knowledge not only about the Florida crab business, but also about the Chesapeake Bay; and Pableaux Johnson, who always seemed to know when to call from his Louisiana home and give me a kick in the butt. A special thanks to Jordy Rosenhek, manager of Wild Edibles at Grand Central Terminal in New York City. His help and patience were beyond the call. And a big thank-you to all the chefs and home cooks whose recipes you'll find between these covers.

Without the great folks at The Harvard Common Press none of this could ever have been possible. They are such wonderful people to be partnered with in a project like this. And thank you to Brian Hagiwara for the wonderful photographs and to Barbara Balch, who shaped the vision of this book.

I'd be remiss not to mention Toni Allegro, a great person, a great teacher, and a great inspiration. Without her positive attitude, I doubt I would ever have written a thing.

INTRODUCTION

Crabmeat got me into trouble as a child. I was about 10 years old when I discovered the magical essence of crab. The problem came as I ate more than my share of crab claws at a cocktail party in Myrtle Beach, South Carolina. I was like a buzzard, swooping down on the bowl of claws and hightailing it like crazy. I couldn't help myself; those claws were just too good. I risked punishment and banishment with each raid, as my embarrassed father railed at me to stay away from the food. Finally, my parents' good friend Blanche Brown, the hostess, came to my rescue and sat me down in the kitchen with my own personal bowl of claws. So started a 30-plus-year love of the most cantankerous beast in the sea.

There's a saying about blue crabs that I suspect applies to the entire species: "Put one crab in a bushel basket, and it will find a way to climb out. Put two in a basket, and they'll fight each other so that neither will escape." Crabs love to fight—with each other and with us. The task of getting that luscious crab to the table can be difficult, but the end result is always well worth the effort.

Crabs have been very regional in nature until the past few years. Improved transportation has given seafood wholesalers the ability to make crabmeat—and different crab types—available on a more widespread basis, challenging some regional preferences along the way. The blue crab's primary domain has long been considered the Chesapeake Bay. Folks along the eastern and western shores of the bay will quickly tell you that the Chesapeake blue crab and the methods they use to prepare the beast are superior to any other. The blue crab does exist elsewhere, though, in the sounds and bays along the Atlantic coast and in the Gulf of Mexico. People in these areas are just as proud of their crabs and the recipes that they have applied to them for decades. From the north coast of California to the cold waters of Alaska, another, larger crustacean holds court: the Dungeness crab. Sweeter, denser, and more meat with less trouble are the battle cries of the Dungeness troops. And what of King crabs and Jonahs, snow crabs, and the newly named peekytoe crab, which is really a rock or sand crab? Their fine taste also demands respect.

I should confess that I grew up on the East Coast, a few hours west of the blue crab–rich estuaries of North Carolina. For more than half my life, the only "fitting" crabmeat came from a blue crab. The imported canned Dungeness crab that was available was poorly packed and contained more water than crab. Over time, I journeyed to the crab meccas of the East Coast: Faidley's in Baltimore's Lexington Market; the Crab Claw Restaurant in St. Michaels, Maryland; crab feasts in Crab City, aka Annapolis, Maryland; the National Hard Crab Derby & Fair in Crisfield, Maryland, the self-proclaimed Crab Capital of the World; Urbanna, Virginia, home to some of the best softshell crabs in the Chesapeake Bay; and the crabbers' enclave on King Street in Hampton, Virginia. I thought I knew crabs.

Then 2 years ago, I hunkered down on one of the stools at Swan Oyster Depot in San Francisco and was treated to not only divine Dungeness crab Louis but also to an education on West Coast crabs. Maybe all this crab business deserved another look.

"Follow the water," veteran crabbers say. A simple thought, easily spoken. Yet for a waterman on the Chesapeake Bay, a crabber in the sounds of North Carolina or the Pacific Northwest, or anyone who brings the treasures of crab to our tables, this is the gospel, verse, and truth. When William W. Warner first published his Pulitzer Prize–winning book *Beautiful Swimmers: Watermen, Crabs and the Chesapeake Bay* in 1976, he opened the door to a region and an industry largely unknown to most Americans. Although his book focused on the Chesapeake Bay, he indirectly paid tribute to all those people, from all areas of the country, who heroically provide crab and fish for our culinary pleasure.

Pat Whewell, a trotliner out of Tongers Basin on Tilghman Island in the Chesapeake Bay, has been crabbing for 20-plus years. He's up at 3:00 A.M. and on the water by 3:30. His day on the bay ends by early afternoon, his catch sold. Then he returns to Tongers Basin to prepare his boat for the next day. If time permits and the day has been successful, he might drink "coffee" (think alcoholic beverage) with other watermen at the small general store. He wonders about his future and the future of blue crabs in the Bay. He's not alone.

Wayne Bridges, manager of the exceptional Crab Claw Restaurant and a lifetime resident of the area, is concerned that the crab might go the way of the oyster, once the biggest source of income on the bay. Rockfish, which are prevalent in the bay, have been protected and now gorge themselves with young crabs at an alarming rate. Is there a balance?

Three thousand miles away, just outside Fort Bragg, California, Frank Bertoni could not be any more different from Pat Whewell, yet both are very much of the same mind. Bertoni crabs with specially designed pots he makes himself. He has been crabbing for almost 50 years, but he would consider only 5 of those years great. Bertoni looks at the ocean as a bank: "You take just what you need and return what you don't. If you fish like that, the ocean will look out for you." Both Bertoni and Whewell are concerned about government regulations and that seem to them to favor the large outfitters. Bertoni has seen large boats arrive in the San Francisco area with more Dungeness crabs than could be processed, resulting in 5,000 to 6,000 pounds of crabs left to die, wasted.

Crabs are strange creatures. Their habits seem set, then will change completely. Watermen and crabbers are in tune with these changes. They have a sense—stronger than a sixth sense—almost a mystical ability to understand the variances of crabs and the water. Pat Whewell says simply, "You can't fight the water."

Beth Thomas, educational coordinator at the Baruch Marine Field Laboratory, part of the University of South Carolina and located at Hobcaw Barony in Winyah Bay, near Georgetown, South Carolina, has an interesting insight: "If you are a lover of seafood, then remember that you can trace almost every seafood species back to the salt marshes, where they begin life and grow." Although East Coast crabs are being invaded by scrappy species from the waters of China and Japan, their biggest threat is from the "encroaching development in the watersheds." To eat, we must conserve. As you travel the coastal regions of our country, talk with the folks who fill your plate. We sometimes forget where our food was before it hit the supermarket shelf or refrigerator case, and that continued myopia, my friends, will end up hurting us.

In using this cookbook, you will find a mixture of old ways of cooking crab mingled with newfangled flavors and methods. No matter what the crab—Dungeness, blue, king, or Jonah—its flesh beckons you with its singular rich flavor and incomparable texture. Crab is a culinary crown prince that enjoys playing with other flavors, but by itself crab is a feast for the tongue and the soul.

THE Crab BASICS

Crabs have become the national crustacean. Once a regional delicacy, crab is now everywhere: king and snow crab clusters will fill a restaurant in Kansas; Dungeness crab is found in supermarkets on the Eastern Shore of the Delmarva Peninsula, the land of steamed blue crabs; and soft-shell crabs, once limited to the East Coast, have exploded in popularity, with fans as far away as California.

Several species of crab are available in the United States: blue crab, Dungeness crab, Alaskan king crab, snow crab, Jonah crab, rock crab, and stone crab. These are the major players and the ones this book will deal with. They are also the ones most likely to show up in your market. With improved cold storage and overnight air delivery, you may have access to many, if not all, of them. If your choices are more limited, worry not. Crab, in any species, is a sweet, rich taste experience, and it is perfectly permissible to substitute just about any crab for another in most of the recipes in this book.

Let's take a look at these crabs, so that you'll understand some of the crab terminology you will run up against at the grocer, fishmonger, or your local pier.

BLue crabs

The beauty of blue crabs is how easy they can be to catch. A stout line, a chicken neck, a homemade net, and you're ready for crabbing. Blue crabs (*Callinectes sapidus*) reside in the waters along the eastern seaboard from Rhode Island to the tip of Florida, around the peninsula, and throughout the Gulf of Mexico. Blue crabs like shallow water and are most abundant in rivers, sounds, and bays. That's why it is so easy to go down to the end of a pier and catch dinner. No boat is required. The watermen of the Chesapeake Bay have a name for those weekend folks and vacationing families who explore the bounty of the water: chicken neckers. If only commercial crabbing were that easy.

Commercial crabbing for blues usually takes one of two forms—crab pots and trotlines. Most of us are familiar with crab pots, which look something like a box of chicken wire with funnels. Crabs are easily enticed into the pots, but getting out is pretty near impossible. Watermen, as they are known in the Chesapeake Bay (crabbers elsewhere), will lay out hundreds of these traps, each attached to a float painted with what appears to be pure whimsy but in reality is the owner's mark, signifying that his pot hangs below. The second type of crabbing is known as trotline crabbing. Trotlines are long lines that are baited at intervals and anchored at both ends. Salted chicken necks or veal or beef lips are popular baits. Each party swears by its particular method. Some crab-eating folks claim that trotline crabs taste better. There is a third method of crabbing, called scraping, which is used when crabs have embedded themselves in the sandy bottom. Scraping relies on a kind of underwater plow with a net to capture the crabs as they pop out of the bottom. Some older watermen and crabbers don't care much for this method, and the debate over its use goes on. However, this method is best for harvesting peelers—crabs that will soon be soft-shell crabs.

Blue crabs account for 50 to 70 percent (depending on whom you ask) of the crab consumed in this country. People in the Chesapeake Bay region claim that half of those crabs come from their waters, but the crab population in the bay has been low for several years. In North Carolina, where most residents believe that the shrimp is king of the seafood business, it is actually the blue crab that leads the pack. North Carolina crabbers now supply many of the picking houses in Maryland and Virginia with crabs. Other important blue crab regions can be found in South Carolina, Georgia, Florida, Louisiana, and Texas. Blue crab season runs from about May to October.

Blue crabs come to market live. Dead crabs have no place in the culinary world. Crabs are mean and feisty, so handle them with care. Use tongs or heavy gloves when dealing with a live blue crab. The best way to judge a live crab is by how active it is. Activity is a good sign of a fresh, good-tasting crab. There are many categories of blue crabs in the commercial crab business—hard, soft, peelers, greens, buckrams, and busters, among others, but you need to be concerned only with sooks, jimmies, and softs.

SOOKS AND JIMMIES

A *sook* is a female blue crab, which is easily identified by the dome-shaped apron resembling the U.S. Capitol on its underbelly. A she-crab is a mature female crab. If a fishmonger tells you that his females are sponge crabs, that means they are carrying egg masses, which is not a bad thing, especially if she-crab soup (see pages 73 and 74) is on the menu. Sooks tend to have less meat than male crabs and usually end up in the picking plants for crabmeat.

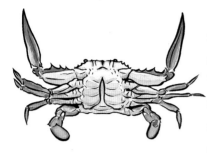

A *jimmy*, as the name implies, is a male crab. Whereas the female has the Capitol dome as part of its anatomy, a jimmy, not to be outdone, can be spotted by an apron that looks a lot like the Washington Monument. Prized for the amount of meat they can contain, jimmies are the blue crabs of summer. A number one size jimmy (the biggest) is a pure pleasure to eat after it has been perfectly steamed or boiled. Most large jimmies are sold whole, either live or steamed.

SOFTS or SOFT-SHELL CRabS

These are crabs that have molted—broken free from their shells—so that they can continue their growth cycle. They are removed from the water as soon as they molt to prevent any hardening of the shell. Softs are eaten whole—legs, claws, crunchy shells, and all. Soft-shell crabs have become a market phenomenon in recent decades and can now be found throughout the country, at least in restaurants. Beginning in late March, when soft-shell season opens in Florida, the East Coast becomes stupefied with softs. There is intense competition to be the first restaurant in the area with a soft-shell dish on the menu. Up and down the East Coast, soft shells are a welcome sight to those who have longed for them since the end of the previous summer, when fresh soft shells vanish. Soft-shell crab marketing, which is less than 100 years old, has resulted in one of the largest seafood industries in the Chesapeake Bay region.

Softs are sold live, fresh dressed (cleaned), or dressed and frozen. No matter what their form, soft-shell crabs are graded and named according to size. *Mediums* are 2½ to 4 inches, *hotels* are 4 to 4½ inches, *primes* are 4½ to 5 inches, *jumbos* are 5 to 5½ inches, and *whales* are more than 5½ inches. All of these sizes have a place, but when buying softs for home, I like hotels and primes. They are a little sweeter and easier to deal with in home-style cooking.

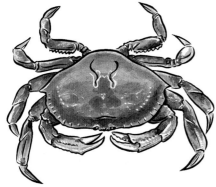

Cancer magister: even in Latin the Dungeness crab makes its importance known. This reddish brown crab is the centerpiece of the West Coast shellfish industry. Dungeness crabs can be found from Santa Barbara, California, to the Pribilof Islands of Alaska. The San Francisco Bay area has a long history of commercially landing Dungeness crabs, but the consensus is that this industry began on the Strait of Juan de Fuca, off the coast of Washington.

Dungeness crab season typically starts in late fall and runs until early spring, but the winter months are most productive. Alaskan Dungeness season runs into the summer, making this crab nearly a year-round treat in the Pacific Northwest. Most Dungeness crab is sold cooked, whole, cracked, portioned, picked, or frozen. Some live Dungeness crabs are available during the crabbing season, especially on the West Coast and in large Asian communities, but by and large, you'll find Dungeness already cooked. Dungeness crab is now available nationally. I bought frozen Dungeness clusters in a supermarket in eastern North Carolina and found them to be of acceptable quality.

Dungeness crabs weigh on average 2 to 3 pounds, with 25 percent of that weight being meat. Only males of a certain size can be taken, and females are left to reproduce. These crabs are caught in circular pots that are much sturdier than those meant for blue crabs. This is because Dungeness crabs prefer deep water and the winter seas can get fairly rough. Although Dungeness crabs do molt, soft-shell Dungeness crabs have not been marketed successfully.

KING CRABS AND SNOW CRABS

If you have eaten at a seafood buffet, you are familiar with these two critters. *Alaskan king crab* is a broad term applied to all king crab species. The red king crab (*Paralithodes camtschatica*) is the most common and abundant, but there are also blue (*Paralithodes platypus*) and brown (*Lithodes aequispina*) varieties. As opposed to blue and Dungeness crabs, which have 10 legs, king crabs have 6 legs with 2 claws. They are large, averaging 10 pounds or more.

King crabs are found in the super-cold waters off Alaska at a depth of about one-half mile. Kings are caught in pots and kept alive in tanks aboard boats that are generally 100 feet or more long. Most of the catch is frozen as legs and claws, making king crab available all year long. The bodies are almost never brought to market, but the backfin meat is canned. I have run across frozen picked king crab on rare occasions, but, frankly, buying it this way takes all the fun out of eating king crabs.

Snow crabs (*Chionoecetes opilio* or *C. bairdi*) are found in the Atlantic and Pacific Oceans, especially off the coasts of Canada and Alaska. Called opies by fishermen, snow crabs are smaller than kings, and their bodies are covered with dense, fuzzy hair. They average about 5 pounds. Snow crabs get their name from the pristine color of their meat. Virtually all snow crab is shipped frozen. Legs and clusters are the most popular items, but picked snow crab is also available frozen. The Canadian season for snow crabs is April through November. In the Bering Sea, the start of the season depends on when the ice breaks, and the season extends through the summer months.

stone crabs

Stone crabs (*Menippe mercenaria*) are found mainly along the coast of Florida and as far north as North Carolina. We eat only the claws of the stone crab, and the meat is sweet and dense—in the opinion of some, like lobster. Stone crabs are trapped, with as many as 400 traps on a single line. Only 1 claw is taken from each crab, then the crab is returned to the sea to regenerate another claw. The claw has to be removed with exact precision, and the length of the claw is regulated. Egg-bearing females must be returned to the water intact. Stone crabbing is highly regulated in Florida, where being in possession of a whole stone crab, even a dead one, is illegal. The season for stone crabs is mid-October to mid-May. Stone crab claws are always sold cooked and usually are frozen, making them available year-round. They are great cracked and served chilled (with mustard sauce, of course) or slightly warm. You can pick their meat to use in recipes with exceptional results.

a word about surimi

This fake crab product, developed in Japan, is cooked white fish that has been flavored, colored, and compressed into chunks. It has its place. After all, what would a California roll be without it? You can use surimi in the salad recipes in this book, but use the real stuff in crab cakes, soups, and casseroles, which just aren't the same prepared with surimi.

maine crabs

The Gulf of Maine has long been a shellfish bonanza, but its main product was always lobster. Crabs got in the way, and their availability was a byproduct of lobstering. Not anymore. Twenty years ago, as the demand for crabmeat outstripped the supply, the Jonah crab (*Cancer borealis*) made its debut. A deep-water crab, the Jonah is a very close cousin of the Pacific Dungeness crab. It is slightly smaller, but the meat is sweet, though maybe not quite as rich as Dungeness. In cooked dishes, however, it is hard to tell them apart. Jonahs are cheaper than Dungeness crabs, so many East Coast tanks that once were full of Dungeness crabs now hold only Jonahs. Many Chinatown restaurants routinely use Jonah crabs. Live Jonahs are widely available through mail-order sources, and buyers can treat them exactly as they would Dungeness crabs. Picked Jonah crabmeat, usually labeled Maine crabmeat, is becoming much more widespread. Generally, Maine crabmeat is much less expensive than Dungeness and picked blue crab.

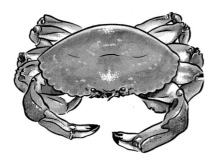

In what must be one of the great marketing coups of all time, the lowly rock or sand crab (*Cancer irroratus*) became the peekytoe crab. Peekytoe crabmeat is highly sought after by some of the most famous and discriminating chefs around the world. These crabs are harvested year-round in waters that are 20 to 40 feet deep and weigh only about 1 pound each. They spoil quickly. Their meat is very moist and delicate in texture and fresh in flavor. For the most part, peekytoe crab is used in salads and very simply prepared dishes, so the flavor of the crab stands out. Many restaurants use peekytoe in crab cakes, noting its cheaper-than-blue-crab price and the lovely menu-speak it creates.

Why "peekytoe"? That's local slang for these crabs, which have legs with a very sharp point that turns slightly inward. "Picked" is Maine-speak for pointed, thus "picked toe" or "peekytoe." Peekytoe crabs cannot be shipped live because they are so perishable. The cooking and picking of peekytoe crabs is still a cottage industry carried out by the wives of lobstermen. What started in their kitchens is now done in FDA-approved buildings constructed next to their homes. The talent of pickers varies from house to house, and high-profile chefs have their favorites. Thomas Keller of the French Laundry in Yountville, California, arguably the finest restaurant in the country, requests that his favorite picker sign each container she picks and packs for him. If you can find peekytoe in your area, you owe it to yourself to give this crab a try.

Both Jonah and peekytoe crabs are trapped in pots, some much like lobster traps, and are harvested through the summer and early fall.

portioning a dungeness crab

many recipes calling for a precooked Dungeness crab ask for it to be "cleaned and portioned." Most of the time, your fishmonger will do this for you, or you can buy the portions ready to go. If you have to accomplish this task yourself, it is fairly simple. Remove the top shell and clean the innards out as suggested in How to Pick a Cooked Crab on page 28. Break or cut the crab in half, then break or cut those pieces in half. You'll end up with 4 portions, each containing legs and body meat.

Buying and Storing Crabs and Crab Products

W hen you step up to your favorite seafood counter, the choice of crab products may seem daunting. Go to a coastal region, and that confusion likely will multiply. A little knowledge can go a long way in selecting the best crab product for your intended use.

Live Crabs

A good rule of thumb from crab country is "If the crab ain't kicking, he ain't cooking." No truer words could be said. Blue, Dungeness, and Jonah crabs are those most likely to be sold live. Let your senses and common sense guide you in your purchase.

Blues usually are sorted by sooks and jimmies (see page 13), but not always, so check a few underbellies for the "Capitol dome" or "Washington Monument." Blues are also sold right from the bushel basket they came to market in. Blues are tough fellows, and a day or two out of the water is fine for them. But ask questions as to when the delivery was made and where the crabs came from. Make sure that each crab you or your fishmonger chooses reacts to being picked up and is very active. If not, the crab may be close to death, and you should choose another. Remember, the blues you have purchased are living creatures and need air. Most markets package live crabs in brown paper bags, which is perfect. If your crabs are put in a plastic bag, be sure to poke a few holes in it. If it's warm out, ask for some ice to help keep them cool until you get home. Store them in a loosely closed paper bag in the lower part of your refrigerator. Cook the crabs the same day you buy them if possible, but you can hold them for 24 hours if necessary. The chill will make them subdued, but when you cook them, they should put up a mild fuss when they sense the heat. Discard any that don't.

Live Dungeness and Jonah crabs are sold from a saltwater tank. Once a crab is put in this environment, it stops feeding, and the ratio of meat to shell starts to decrease. Again, ask about where the crabs came from and how long they have been in the tank. Remember to let them breathe, and don't let them lounge in water or ice. Try to cook these crabs the day you buy them. If not, put a damp towel over the crabs in their bag and definitely cook them the next day.

If you want to use Dungeness or Jonah crab in a dish such as a stir-fry, I highly recommend that you have your fishmonger clean the crab. Actually, it's more than a recommendation; just have him do it. You won't regret it; this is not a fun job.

cooked whole crabs

You are much more likely to see Dungeness and Jonah crabs sold cooked. These crabs are usually cooked within hours of being landed, so the loss of flavor is minimal. Some are then frozen; others are shipped refrigerated. Blue crabs also are sold in some markets already steamed, complete with Chesapeake Bay seasoning (see page 35). Cooked whole crabs should be displayed on ice or in a refrigerated case. Talk with your fishmonger about when the crabs were cooked. You want to consume the crab within 3 to 4 days of its being cooked. Look each crab over for cracks in the shell, make sure all the legs and claws are in place, and even shake the crab slightly and listen for water. There's no sense in paying crab prices for water. The test of a good seafood market is if the fishmonger will let you taste a leg. Not all will, but it never hurts to ask. Finally, your nose is a great tool when shopping for seafood. If a market smells of ammonia, leave. If you get a faint whiff of ammonia from a single crab, choose another.

Frozen Cooked Crabs and Crab Parts

King and snow crab legs or leg clusters, stone crab claws, snow crab cocktail claws, and whole Dungeness and Jonah crabs are sold frozen. According to Gene Mattiuzzo of Caito Fisheries in Northern California, frozen crab products have a shelf life of 4 to 6 months before they start to lose flavor or texture. That, of course, assumes that the crab has been handled properly by the processor and in its journey to your freezer. Unfortunately, that doesn't happen very often. Crab that has been allowed to thaw slightly and is then refrozen loses taste and texture quickly. When buying bags of legs and claws, as well as individual whole crabs, look for telltale signs of bad handling. An ice glaze on the product is fine, but frost and ice crystals in the bag are not. Also look for areas of freezer burn or oxidation, which is brownish to gray in color. Look for it at the top of the legs or leg clusters, where the meat is exposed. This is a sure sign of age or mishandling.

Make sure to thaw your frozen crab in the refrigerator. Cynthia Nims, the former editor of *Simply Seafood* magazine, warns that frozen crab products release a lot of water during the thawing process. Thaw your crab in a baking dish to catch the fluid, keeping your refrigerator tidy.

Slightly crack the shells of all precooked crab products if you are going to cook them further. This allows additional flavors to penetrate the meat.

Soft-Shell Crabs

Soft shells are a wonderful treat when handled properly. Soft-shell crabs are sold live, fresh dressed (cleaned), and dressed and frozen. Live soft shells are packed in layers separated by eelgrass and are shipped for quick sale. Since these crabs have molted, which is stressful for the crabs, they are very docile. Some may *look* dead, while others actually are dead. Look for motion and bubbles around the face.

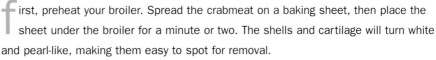

Blow gently on the crabs and see if they stir, or touch them (or have your fishmonger do so). Soft-shell crabs are highly perishable. Again, when buying soft shells, question, question, question.

You can clean soft-shell crabs easily at home (see page 30), but if you are squeamish, have your fishmonger do the deed. I am very suspicious of buying dressed soft shells that have not been frozen. Cleaning soft shells right before cooking results in the best taste. A chef friend of mine, Bret Jennings, who does killer soft shells in his restaurant, cleans his crabs to order. (Don't miss his recipe on page 141.) Cook your soft shells the day you buy them for the best results.

Frozen soft shells are okay, although they do lose some of that magnificent flavor of a fresh, live crab. The best use for frozen soft shells is to fry them. Once you've had a good fried soft-shell sandwich, you'll understand the necessity of having the frozen product. Frozen soft-shell crabs also add flavor to soups and stews. But stay away from grilling or sautéing frozen soft shells. Always let frozen softs thaw completely in the refrigerator before using.

PICKED CRAB OR CRABMEAT

Crabmeat is sold "fresh," pasteurized, frozen, and canned. "Fresh" crabmeat is lightly cooked, either boiled or steamed, to release the meat from its shell.

Pasteurized crabmeat goes through an additional process to extend its shelf life. Frozen crabmeat is cooked crab that is quick-frozen after it is removed from its shell. Canned crabmeat has been cooked and processed more than any other crabmeat. Read the label and look for the smallest number of ingredients.

I used to be a snob when it came to crabmeat, insisting on only "fresh." But I have found good processors of pasteurized meat, and Dungeness crab fares well with a vacuum-packed canning process. Generally, I've been disappointed with imported crabmeat, which accounts for most canned crab. The texture is often subpar and the taste subdued. Read the labels carefully; some American companies use imported meat. And don't pay "fresh" prices for pasteurized meat. Just because it's displayed on ice does not guarantee that the crabmeat is fresh.

The best cooking method for picked crab is an ongoing debate. Maryland blue crabmeat, which has gained a reputation as the best, is steamed. Most processors in Louisiana, which provides this country with beaucoup blue crabmeat, boil it. Dungeness crab is almost always boiled. Does boiling make a difference? Boiled meat may be a little softer in texture than steamed meat, but there is so little difference in usability to the home cook that the processing method is more a matter of regional pride than of quality. More important is the packer's reputation for freshness and the percentage of shells and cartilage mixed in with the meat.

After you pass the hurdle of "fresh," pasteurized, frozen, or canned, you are confronted by another question: what grade? This is primarily a blue crab phenomenon, since the picked meat of other crabs is either mixed body and leg meat or all leg meat. Blue crab, however, is graded and sold according to the size of the chunk of meat, or "lump."

Jumbo lump backfin: This is the Cadillac of crabmeat. It consists of large white chunks of meat with very few shells or cartilage. This style

is best used in salads where very little is done to the meat. I would not use it in a casserole or for most hors d'oeuvres. If you make crab cakes with this grade, don't deep-fry them. Instead, gently pan-fry or broil them to enjoy the crab's full flavor and texture. My favorite preparation with this superior crabmeat is Crab Norfolk (page 184), where taste, texture, and appearance are important, although I would not hesitate to use another grade there as well.

Backfin: Backfin crab, sometimes referred to as lump backfin, comes from the rear fin area of the crab and contains some large pieces of meat as well as broken or smaller chunks. Typically, there are more shells and cartilage mixed in with backfin than with jumbo lump. This grade of crabmeat is the workhorse of blue crabmeat. It is appropriate for most recipes and makes a fine crab cake. Backfin is usually $5 to $6 a pound cheaper than jumbo lump.

Special: Special crabmeat includes meat from all parts of the crab: legs, claws, and body. The pieces are much smaller, sometimes referred to as flaked, and there are considerably more shells and cartilage intermingled with the meat. It makes a good crab cake (maybe not a pretty one) and is good in casseroles, dips, and soups. Many people use special crabmeat to extend the more costly backfin or jumbo lump. Special and backfin or jumbo lump in combination make a great crab cake, as the sweetness that special retains from having claw meat in the mix adds to the overall flavor. Special crabmeat is usually the least expensive of the grades.

Claw meat: I love claw meat for its firm texture and strong crab flavor. Unfortunately, the meat is reddish brown, which isn't appealing in many dishes. It is superb in soups and stews, casseroles, and dips. When testing my crab cake recipes, many of the tasters preferred the flavor of claw meat over higher grades. You can mix claw meat with other crabmeat grades to achieve a balance of flavor and visual appeal. Be sure to pick it over for shells and cartilage.

Smith Island Special Deluxe: Smith Island is one of the many islands in the Chesapeake Bay with a long history and tradition in the crab business. You will find this grade only in the Chesapeake region, and it is the favorite of the locals. Just like regular special crabmeat, it contains both body and claw meat. It is well picked and handled gently, resulting in some nice chunks. Smith Island Special Deluxe is the best of all worlds. Although some seafood wholesalers will freeze this crabmeat and ship it to you, if you get the chance to eat it fresh, dive in.

Cocktail claws: A cocktail claw is the last segment of the claw with most of the shell removed except for the pinchers, making it perfect for dipping. Blue crab claws are prepared this way, as are the larger snow crab claws. They are sold fresh, pasteurized, and canned (blue crab) or frozen (snow crab). My first taste of crab was a blue crab claw, and I've been hooked ever since. Cocktail claws are awesome party food and make one damn good snack.

Other crabmeat: Picked Dungeness, Jonah, and peekytoe crabs are sold in combinations of body, leg, and claw meat. They tend to have only small amounts of shells and cartilage. Dungeness and Jonah crabmeat can be used in almost any preparation. I like Dungeness simply prepared, eaten cold or in a salad, but don't stop there. Dungeness and Jonah are both outstanding in crab cakes and most casseroles. Peekytoe is a delicate crab, and its flavor is best appreciated in salads and very simple, not highly seasoned presentations. Even the great chefs treat peekytoe with a light hand. I have had extraordinary crab cakes made with peekytoe.

King, snow, and stone crabs are sometimes available picked. Normally, they are found frozen and are usually flaked, with little chunk meat. Use this crabmeat for hors d'oeuvres, dips, and soups. For me, eating these crabs this way takes all the fun out of struggling with their shells.

the grades of crabmeat used in this book

In many of the recipes in this book, you will not find a grade or species of crabmeat specified. These recipes work with any crabmeat. Crab Imperial, for example, can be a success prepared with Dungeness, king, stone, or Maine crabmeat, as well as the more traditional blue crab. Crab Louis works well with lump blue crab, as well as the usual Dungeness. The idea is to use the best-quality crabmeat available no matter where you live. Also, with a few exceptions, I want to put you in control of your pocketbook. Yes, high-end restaurants love jumbo lump backfin crabmeat, but is the most expensive crabmeat really appropriate for you and your family? In this chapter, I've given you some suggestions about which types of dishes work best with each grade of crabmeat. The rest is up to you.

Storing crabmeat depends on which type of product you buy. Obviously, if the product is frozen, store it that way and thaw it in the refrigerator. For fresh crabmeat, store it on ice or in the coldest part of your refrigerator. Use fresh crabmeat within a couple of days. Your nose is your best guide to quality. Refrigerated pasteurized crabmeat should be stored in the refrigerator's coldest area; use it before its "use by" date. Once opened, use it within a couple of days. Again, your nose is your friend. All crabmeat should be well drained before using it in any recipe.

HOW TO PICK a COOKED CraB

For years, I was afraid, even embarrassed, to order steamed or boiled crabs in a restaurant, even though I love crabmeat. I thought there was a secret way to pick crabs that I didn't know. Please don't make that mistake. There really is no right or wrong way to pick a crab, but there are some basic techniques to make sure you get as much of the creamy meat as possible. The method is pretty much the same for blue and Dungeness crabs. You don't need any special equipment, although claw crackers will help and a mallet is useful. You may need a heavy knife for Dungeness crabs, depending on your strength.

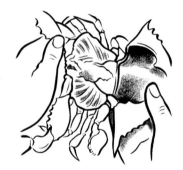

FIG. 1

1. Flip the crab over so the apron is exposed. With a knife or your thumb, pop off the apron.

2. Turn the crab over and pry off the top shell. *(See Fig. 1.)* This is where you may go "ugh," because the innards will be hanging off the shell. Ignore them and soldier on.

FIG. 2

3. Scrape or pull off the gray-colored spongy gills, which are called dead man's fingers. *(See Fig. 2.)* Scrape out the rest of the innards, called the devil. The yellow stuff you'll find is called the mustard, which is the crab's fat and quite good. I usually let it mingle with the meat.

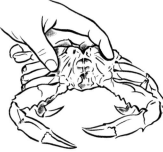

FIG. 3

FIG. 4

4. Break the crab in half. Gently push down on the back of the shell where the back (rear) flipper legs are located. *(See Fig. 3.)* This will loosen the big chunks of meat.

5. Break the legs and claws off the body. *(See Fig. 4.)* There will be a small piece of meat on each leg. Eat it and reserve the claws. We'll get to them later.

6. Every place where the legs are connected to the body is a cavity full of meat. Use your fingers or a small knife to get at it.

7. Break the joints around the claws. Using crackers or a mallet, crack the claws. Notice I said crack; don't pound the claws to pieces. Remove the meat.

8. Repeat until the crabs are gone or you can hold no more.

---

making the most of crab legs

When faced with a pile of king crab legs or snow crab clusters, first look for cracks or slits that the processor may have made to help you get started. These are the best places to begin cracking and breaking open the legs. If that hasn't been done, use lobster crackers to start gently popping the legs. The meat will release pretty easily, except for those stubborn tiny legs. I wish I could give you the perfect method for them, but patience is the only virtue. There is lots of good lump meat at the top of the legs, where they are attached to the body. I like to take a spoon, turn it around, and use the handle end to scoop out the meat.

HOW TO CLEAN (DRESS) a SOFT-SHELL CRAB

Most fishmongers will clean your soft shells for you, but it's easy to do yourself, and they taste better if cleaned just before cooking. A pair of scissors is the only tool you need.

1. Rinse the crab in cold water. With your scissors, make a cut about ¼ inch behind the eyes. The crab is now dead.

2. Squeeze the crab right behind where you made the cut. This forces out the innards through the cut you just made.

3. Turn the crab over and cut off the apron. Lift up one side of the top shell and scrape off the gray gills with your scissors, or just pull them out. Repeat with the other side. The crab is now ready to cook.

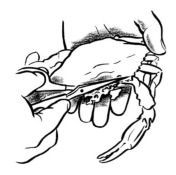

FIG. 1

FIG. 2

FIG. 3

about the recipes

Here are some guidelines for following the recipes in this book. First, let's look at the ingredients.

- I like to use kosher salt for cooking, except when baking. If you use regular table salt, use less.
- Always use unsalted butter. That way, you control the seasoning.
- Grind your pepper fresh, as it adds much more flavor that way.
- If you have never bought whole nutmeg and grated it fresh, please try it. It tastes far superior to the ground kind.
- Use your favorite mayonnaise, but be aware that the recipes were tested with Duke's and JFG. Both contain little or no sugar, making the mayonnaise more lemony. If those brands are not available in your area, read the labels of the ones that are and pick the one containing the least amount of sugar. Homemade mayonnaise is always a good choice.
- Use only freshly squeezed citrus juices.

Second, to *fold* means to stir gently from the bottom of the bowl, bringing the ingredients there up to the top. Mixing crabmeat in this way will keep the larger pieces intact.

Finally, make these recipes your own. Don't hesitate to make adjustments for your personal tastes.

crab WITH cocktails

Want to be the star of a covered-dish party or known as that exquisite gala giver? Then bring on the crab finger foods. Most crab hors d'oeuvres are incredibly easy to put together and the praise they receive is justly deserved. So let's party!

There are so many party possibilities made with crabmeat that you could write a whole book just on crab dips, canapés, and other hors d'oeuvres. In this chapter, you will find a wide variety of ways to introduce the elegance and richness of crab to any gathering you might be hosting or attending. There are simple dips and chafing dish spreads, mini crab cakes, even crab critters. You'll soon find that if you have a pound of crabmeat, you have something to celebrate.

Many of the recipes in this chapter are forgiving enough that you can use whatever variety and price level of crabmeat you choose.

crabmeat canapés

¼ pound crabmeat, lump
    preferred, picked over for
    shells and cartilage

2 tablespoons mayonnaise

1 tablespoon fresh lemon juice

2 tablespoons finely chopped
    celery

2 tablespoons seeded and finely
    chopped green bell pepper

2 hard-boiled large eggs, peeled
    and finely chopped

½ teaspoon Tabasco sauce

¼ teaspoon paprika

8 slices homemade-type white
    bread, crusts removed, each
    slice cut into 4 triangles, and
    toasted

2 tablespoons unsalted butter,
    melted

2 tablespoons fine fresh bread
    crumbs

artinis are back. Cocktail parties are back. Canapés, those cute little finger foods, are back. These canapés are almost like miniature crab gratins and are truly elegant when passed on a silver platter.

SERVES 10 TO 12

1. Preheat broiler.

2. In a medium-size mixing bowl, stir together the crabmeat, mayonnaise, lemon juice, celery, bell pepper, eggs, Tabasco, and paprika until blended well. The crab mixture may be made up to 1 day ahead, covered with plastic wrap, and refrigerated.

3. Spread the crab mixture evenly over the toasts and drizzle with the butter. Sprinkle the bread crumbs evenly on top. Place on a baking sheet and broil about 4 inches from the heat until golden brown, 4 to 5 minutes. Serve hot.

crab-stuffed cherry tomatoes

Cherry tomatoes just burst with flavor during the height of the blue crab season. Stuffing them with crab is truly gilding the lily. These little one-bite goodies are downright sensual. **SERVES 10 TO 12**

1. Slice the stem end off each tomato and set aside. Using a demitasse spoon or your finger, carefully remove about half of the tomato pulp without puncturing the skin. (You can add this to the crab mixture, if you wish, or simply discard it.)

2. Combine the remaining ingredients in a medium-size mixing bowl. Spoon the mixture into a pastry bag fitted with a large round tip and pipe the mixture into the tomato shells, filling them about ½ inch over the top. Or use a small spoon to fill the tomatoes. Set the tomato tops on the crabmeat mixture and serve immediately, or hold in the refrigerator for up to 1 hour.

30 ripe cherry tomatoes, with stems attached if possible, washed and patted dry

½ pound crabmeat, backfin preferred, picked over for shells and cartilage

4 teaspoons sour cream

1 tablespoon chopped fresh Italian parsley leaves

1 tablespoon finely diced yellow onion

½ teaspoon Worcestershire sauce

½ teaspoon Chesapeake Bay seasoning

⅛ teaspoon white pepper

---

what is chesapeake bay seasoning?

Many of the recipes call for Chesapeake Bay seasoning, which has a base of paprika, with salt, black pepper, garlic powder, and cayenne added. Each brand of seasoning is unique. Old Bay, out of Baltimore, is the big gun on the market, and is considered to be the gold standard. J.O. Spice is another Baltimore company with a loyal following. Many crab houses use its #2 blend for steaming crabs. J.O. Spice products are available via mail order on the Internet. Another local favorite is Wye River, out of Queenstown, Maryland. No matter which blend a crab house uses, most will doctor it up a bit to make their crabs taste a little different from the guy's down the road. Make your own (see page 167), use one of the commercial brands, or add something to a store-bought concoction. Whatever you do, you'll have a taste of the Chesapeake Bay.

sam's crab-stuffed mushrooms

Filling:

1 large egg, lightly beaten

1 cup mayonnaise

2 cups dry bread crumbs

½ teaspoon white pepper

1 teaspoon kosher salt

2 tablespoons chopped fresh
Italian parsley leaves

1 pound crabmeat, lump preferred, picked over for shells
and cartilage

50 stuffing-size white or brown
mushrooms, stems removed
and caps wiped with a damp
paper towel

Topping:

½ cup mayonnaise

1 cup heavy cream

Twenty years ago, mushrooms were truly a gourmet item, but now we sometimes forget just how good they really are. Whoever stuffed a mushroom cap with crab should receive the highest of culinary awards. They go together like gin and vermouth. This recipe is a variation of one that has been served at Sam's Steak House in Raleigh, North Carolina, to millions of adoring fans. Poor me, I had to eat a lot of orders to make sure I had this recipe just right. **SERVES 16 TO 18**

1. Preheat the oven to 350°F. Grease 1 or 2 large baking sheets.

2. To make the filling, combine the egg, mayonnaise, bread crumbs, white pepper, salt, and parsley in a large bowl. Gently fold in the crab-meat, keeping it as chunky as possible.

3. Use the mixture to stuff the mushroom caps. Place on the prepared baking sheet(s).

4. To make the topping, combine the mayonnaise and cream in a small bowl, stirring until smooth. Top the stuffed mushrooms with the mixture.

5. Bake until golden brown, 20 to 25 minutes. Serve hot.

Variation: For a twist, add ½ teaspoon Chesapeake Bay seasoning or 1 to 2 tablespoons crumbled cooked bacon to the filling.

Note: Any unused crab stuffing may be frozen until needed.

Japanese Deviled Eggs with Crabmeat

Wasabi, pickled ginger, and rice vinegar give a whole new dimension to the routine deviled egg. Mix in some crabmeat, and people will beg you for the recipe. The wasabi paste, pickled ginger, and vinegar can be found in the Asian section of many large supermarkets. This recipe is easy to double or triple. **SERVES 6**

6 hard-boiled large eggs, cooled

¾ cup crabmeat, picked over for shells and cartilage

2 tablespoons chopped fresh chives

2 tablespoons mayonnaise

1 tablespoon unseasoned rice vinegar

1 teaspoon wasabi paste

Kosher salt and freshly ground black pepper to taste

Sliced pickled ginger

Tamari or other low-sodium soy sauce

1. Peel the eggs, then cut them in half. Remove the yolks and set the whites aside.

2. In a medium-size mixing bowl, combine the egg yolks, crab, chives, mayonnaise, vinegar, and wasabi, mixing with a fork to blend. Season with salt and pepper. Pile the yolk mixture back into the whites, mounding it high.

3. Arrange the eggs on a platter and serve immediately, with the ginger and tamari in little bowls on the side. Or hold in the refrigerator for up to 2 hours before serving.

devil those eggs clean and easy

here's an easy way to get the filling into the eggs. Put it in a zippered-top plastic bag, cut off one corner, and squeeze the filling into the egg halves.

crab-stuffed shrimp

¼ cup finely crushed Club crackers or saltines

3 tablespoons mayonnaise

1 tablespoon chopped fresh Italian parsley leaves

1 teaspoon Dijon mustard

1 teaspoon Worcestershire sauce

1 teaspoon Chesapeake Bay seasoning

1 teaspoon fresh lemon juice

½ pound crabmeat, lump or backfin preferred, picked over for shells and cartilage

16 jumbo shrimp, peeled, deveined, and butterflied

Save this recipe for your favorite friends or a boss whom you need to impress. Crab-stuffed shrimp are not only delicious, but they're also showy. Don't relegate this recipe just to cocktail parties. Three on a plate make a really nice first course. Try your favorite cocktail sauce for dipping.

SERVES 8

1. Preheat the broiler.

2. Mix the crackers, mayonnaise, parsley, mustard, Worcestershire, Bay seasoning, and lemon juice together in a medium-size mixing bowl. Gently fold in the crabmeat. Place some of the crabmeat mixture in the center of each shrimp, then push the cut sides of the shrimp up and around the filling. You can prepare the recipe to this point up to 4 hours in advance and refrigerate.

3. Place the shrimp on a baking sheet lined with aluminum foil and broil until just cooked through, about 5 minutes. Be careful not to overcook. Serve hot.

---

cocktail sauce with a twist

1 cup ketchup

½ cup prepared chili sauce

2 tablespoons prepared horseradish, drained

1 teaspoon Worcestershire sauce

1 teaspoon fresh lemon juice, or to taste

1 teaspoon sugar

½ teaspoon garlic powder

½ teaspoon onion powder

Kosher salt and freshly ground black pepper to taste

Combine all the ingredients in a medium-size mixing bowl. Taste and add more lemon juice, if desired. Cover and refrigerate overnight to let the flavors develop. This will keep for 1 week in the refrigerator. **MAKES JUST SHY OF 2 CUPS**

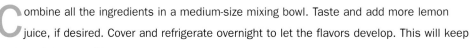

crab spanakopita

The Greeks have had such a great influence on cooking throughout the United States that I had to try using crabmeat in one of the greatest of Greek finger foods—spanakopita. I think the result is special, and I hope you do, too. **MAKES 30 TRIANGLES; SERVES 10 TO 12**

1. Remove the tough stems from the spinach, coarsely chop, and steam for 1 minute. Drain, then wrap in paper towels and squeeze out as much water as possible. Set aside.

2. Chop the garlic. Sprinkle the salt over the garlic and, with the flat part of your knife, rub to form a paste. Set aside.

3. Melt the 1 tablespoon butter in a medium-size skillet over medium-high heat. Add the onion and cook, stirring, until translucent, 3 to 5 minutes. Transfer to a large mixing bowl and let cool.

4. Once the onion has cooled, add the spinach, garlic paste, ricotta, and crab and mix together well. Season to your liking with nutmeg and salt and pepper. Cover with plastic wrap and refrigerate for about 1 hour to let the flavors meld.

5. Preheat the oven to 450°F. Lay out 2 sheets of phyllo on top of each other and cut into 5 strips. Brush the strips with the melted butter. Form 2 tablespoons of the crab mixture into a ball and place it at the bottom of 1 strip. Fold the strip back and forth from corner to corner like a flag. Seal the ends with melted butter. Repeat the process with the remaining strips and then with the remaining sheets of phyllo.

6. Place the triangles on an ungreased baking sheet. Bake until lightly browned, 8 to 10 minutes. Serve hot or at room temperature.

1 pound spinach, washed well

2 cloves garlic, peeled

1 teaspoon kosher salt

1 tablespoon unsalted butter

1 medium-size yellow onion, chopped

1½ pounds ricotta cheese

1 pound crabmeat, backfin preferred, picked over for shells and cartilage

Freshly grated nutmeg to taste

Freshly ground black pepper to taste

6 sheets frozen phyllo dough, defrosted

½ cup (1 stick) unsalted butter, or more if needed, melted

crab-mango cucumber rounds

This is an impressive little canapé that features the flavors of the crab and mango. There's just a little binder and a hint of Asian pizzazz. Use the very best crabmeat you can get or afford. This is also luscious served as a brunch dish on avocado slices. **MAKES 24 TO 30 CANAPÉS; SERVES 10 TO 12 FOR A COCKTAIL PARTY OR 4 AS A BRUNCH DISH**

2 European cucumbers

1 ripe mango, peeled and cut off the pit into small dice

1 cup crabmeat, jumbo lump backfin preferred, picked over for shells and cartilage

1 small jalapeño, seeded and finely diced

1 tablespoon chopped fresh cilantro leaves

1 tablespoon mayonnaise

1 teaspoon toasted sesame oil

Fresh lime juice to taste

Kosher salt to taste

1. Wash the cucumbers. Using a fork, score their sides lengthwise, or peel off thin alternating strips of the peel with a vegetable peeler. Slice into ¼-inch-thick rounds, cover with plastic wrap, and refrigerate until ready to use.

2. Mix the mango, crabmeat, jalapeño, and cilantro together in a medium-size mixing bowl.

3. In a small bowl, whisk the mayonnaise and sesame oil together. Fold the mayonnaise mixture into the crabmeat mixture until every piece is dressed. Taste and add a little lime juice and salt to your liking.

4. Place the cucumber rounds on a baking sheet or serving platter. Put about 1 tablespoon of the crab salad on each round. Serve immediately, or cover with plastic wrap and refrigerate for up to 2 hours.

spinach-crab cheese ball

One 8-ounce package cream
  cheese, softened

4 ounces goat cheese, softened

½ cup washed and finely
  chopped spinach

2 teaspoons prepared horseradish, drained

2 tablespoons minced yellow
  onion

1 tablespoon salad dressing
  (such as Miracle Whip)

⅛ teaspoon freshly grated
  nutmeg

Kosher salt and freshly ground
  black pepper to taste

½ pound crabmeat, picked over
  for shells and cartilage

Sesame crackers

Bon Air Seafood on the south side of Richmond, Virginia, is famous for its shrimp and crab cheese balls. Inspired by those, I threw in a few extra ingredients to elevate this cheese ball to special status. Goat cheese, spinach, and horseradish bring an added dimension to this mixture and will make this cheese ball a hit at your next cocktail party. (P.S. Don't tell anybody about the goat cheese.) **SERVES 12**

1. Blend the cream cheese and goat cheese together in a medium-size mixing bowl. Mix in the spinach, horseradish, onion, salad dressing, nutmeg, and salt and pepper. Fold in the crabmeat.

2. Take two 12×14-inch sheets of plastic wrap and cross them over each other. Put the crab mixture in the middle and pull up on the edges of the wrap to help you form a ball. Tightly twist the top and refrigerate for at least 4 hours. The texture and flavor will improve if you refrigerate overnight.

3. Remove the ball from the plastic, set on a serving platter, and surround with sesame crackers.

Crab and artichokes have been dip-making cousins for quite a while. When I was visiting along the Eastern Shore of Maryland, I found that cheddar cheese is the binder of choice for these folks, but there are as many variations as there are good cooks along the Chesapeake Bay. This inspired version hits pretty close to the wonderful samplings I had in the area. Not only does it make a tasty dip, but add a tossed salad, and you have a nice entrée. **SERVES 16 FOR A COCKTAIL PARTY OR 6 AS A LUNCHEON ENTRÉE**

1. Preheat the oven to 350°F. Butter a 1½-quart casserole.

2. Combine the cheese, mayonnaise, sour cream, mustard, Worcestershire, lemon juice, hot pepper sauce, and black pepper in a large mixing bowl and stir until well mixed. Gently fold in the artichoke hearts, crabmeat, parsley, and chives until well combined. Pour the mixture into the prepared casserole.

3. Bake until hot and bubbly, 20 to 25 minutes. Serve at once with crackers, toasted slices of French bread, or raw vegetables.

½ pound sharp cheddar cheese, shredded

½ cup mayonnaise

½ cup sour cream

1 tablespoon prepared brown mustard

2 teaspoons Worcestershire sauce

2 tablespoons fresh lemon juice

¼ teaspoon hot pepper sauce

Freshly ground black pepper to taste

One 14-ounce jar artichoke hearts, drained (get as much water out as possible) and cut into small pieces

1 pound crabmeat, picked over for shells and cartilage

¼ cup chopped fresh Italian parsley leaves

3 tablespoons chopped fresh chives

stannie's crabmeat dip

Two 8-ounce packages cream
cheese, softened

2 teaspoons prepared horseradish, drained

2 tablespoons minced yellow
onion

2 tablespoons milk

Pinch of kosher salt and freshly
ground black pepper

1 pound crabmeat, backfin
preferred, picked over for
shells and cartilage

Stannie Brewer of Raleigh, North Carolina, may be one of the most out-wardly stress-free people I've met. Even while raising 3 boys, she goes through life with ease and grace. Many of the recipes that she shared with me exemplify that ease. Her crabmeat dip may be one of the simplest and best-tasting recipes in this book. Stannie's original recipe calls for canned crabmeat, which works wonderfully, but I've substituted fresh crabmeat to elevate the flavor even further. If you keep a can of crabmeat and a couple of packages of cream cheese on hand, you can have this wonderful dip in front of unexpected company or friends within 20 minutes. **SERVES 12**

1. Preheat the oven to 350°F.

2. In a large mixing bowl, mix together the cream cheese, horseradish, onion, milk, and salt and pepper, then fold in the crabmeat.

3. Transfer the mixture to a pie plate and bake until bubbling, about 15 minutes.

4. Serve hot with assorted crackers.

THE ABSOLUTE BEST CRAB MOLD

Gelatin and condensed soup in a modern cookbook? Why not? Some things just can't be improved on, and to omit a classic like a crab mold from this book would be unthinkable. You can use goat cheese for an updated flavor, but regular cream cheese will impress your guests just fine.

SERVES 20

1 envelope unflavored gelatin

2 tablespoons water

½ cup condensed cream of mushroom soup

One 8-ounce package cream cheese or goat cheese, softened

1 small yellow onion, finely chopped

1½ cups crabmeat, picked over for shells and cartilage

½ cup finely chopped celery

½ cup mayonnaise

1. Oil a 1-quart mold. Place the gelatin and water in a small bowl and stir to dissolve the gelatin.

2. Heat the soup in a medium-size saucepan over medium-low heat. Stir in the dissolved gelatin, cream cheese, onion, crabmeat, celery, and mayonnaise and blend well. Cook, stirring constantly, until the cheese has melted.

3. Pour the mixture into the prepared mold and let cool. Refrigerate until set, at least 2 hours.

4. Unmold and serve with crackers.

crab picker's spread

1 pound crabmeat, picked over for shells and cartilage

One 0.6-ounce package Italian salad dressing mix

1 cup sour cream

½ cup mayonnaise

1 tablespoon horseradish mustard

Chopped fresh Italian parsley leaves for garnish

I got this recipe from a friend in Richmond, Virginia, but there's probably a variation of it in every Junior League cookbook in the country. This particular one blends the flavors well without covering up the taste of the crab. It's quick, it's simple, and you can use canned crabmeat in a pinch. I particularly like this dip with raw vegetables, but chips and crackers also work fine. **SERVES 20 TO 24**

Combine the crabmeat, salad dressing mix, sour cream, mayonnaise, and mustard in a large mixing bowl. Chill, if desired. Garnish with parsley before serving.

---

chesapeake bay dirty mary

the folks on the Eastern Shore of Maryland and Virginia march to the beat of a different drummer, and I think that drum is filled with Chesapeake Bay crab seasoning. Try this take on a bloody mary. **MAKES 1 DRINK**

1½ ounces vodka

1 tablespoon fresh lemon juice

1 tablespoon Worcestershire sauce

¼ teaspoon Chesapeake Bay seasoning

Pinch of freshly ground black pepper

½ teaspoon prepared horseradish, drained

3 dashes of Tabasco sauce

Tomato-clam juice (such as Clamato)

Celery stick for garnish (optional)

Fill a tall glass with ice. Pour in the vodka, lemon juice, Worcestershire, Bay seasoning, pepper, horseradish, and Tabasco. Stir. Fill the glass with juice, then stir and garnish with a celery stick, if desired.

Greenbrier cooking school crab spread

The Greenbrier hotel and resort in White Sulphur Springs, West Virginia, is one of the last bastions of true Southern hospitality. Every evening, someone puts up a sign in the hallway that declares, "It's sleepy time down South," a sure indication that you are going to be pampered. Long famous for its cuisine, both old style and nouveau spa, the Greenbrier is not satisfied with just feeding you; the staff also wants to teach you how to cook. Rod Stoner, head of food and beverage at the hotel, was one of the chefs when this recipe was developed. He advises being very gentle with the crab when mixing. This crab spread is just as good today as it was when the Greenbrier started serving it 20 years ago. **SERVES 16**

1 pound crabmeat, lump preferred, picked over for shells and cartilage

¼ cup sour cream

¼ cup mayonnaise

2 tablespoons fresh lemon juice

2 tablespoons capers, drained

1 tablespoon celery seeds

Freshly ground black pepper to taste

1. Fold the crabmeat, sour cream, mayonnaise, lemon juice, capers, and celery seeds together in a medium-size mixing bowl. Season to your liking with pepper and stir gently.

2. Serve immediately on crackers, or refrigerate for up to 2 hours before serving.

Baked Seafood Spread

Only those allergic to shellfish won't dive right into this spread made with crab, shrimp, and scallops. You'll find mixed seafood spreads similar to this one up and down the South Carolina coast. I like to use this recipe to help lure people into the kitchen, where I can con them into helping me with a grand Thanksgiving or Christmas dinner. It's kind of like giving them a little reward for their work up front. **SERVES 12**

1. Preheat the oven to 350°F.

2. Melt the butter in a large skillet over medium-high heat. Add the crab, shrimp, and scallops and cook, stirring, just until the shrimp and scallops are opaque all the way through. Be careful not to overcook. Set aside off the heat.

3. In a large mixing bowl, combine the mayonnaise, onion, celery, sherry, mustard, Worcestershire, water, and bread crumbs. Sprinkle with the garlic powder and thyme, if using, and season with salt and pepper. Add the seafood and toss to combine.

4. Transfer the mixture to a small casserole and bake until the top is lightly browned, about 25 minutes.

5. Serve hot with crackers or toasted slices of baguette.

2 tablespoons unsalted butter

½ pound crabmeat, lump preferred, picked over for shells and cartilage

½ pound shrimp, peeled, deveined, and cut into chunks

½ pound bay scallops

1 cup mayonnaise

¼ cup chopped yellow onion

¼ cup chopped celery

¼ cup dry sherry

1 tablespoon Dijon mustard

¼ teaspoon Worcestershire sauce

½ cup water

1 cup dry bread crumbs

⅛ teaspoon garlic powder (optional)

⅛ teaspoon dried thyme (optional)

Kosher salt and freshly ground black pepper to taste

CHESAPEAKE BAY CRAB LOAF

3 tablespoons unsalted butter

1 small yellow onion, finely diced

½ medium-size green bell pepper, seeded and finely diced

1 tablespoon cornstarch

1 cup milk

2 large eggs, lightly beaten

3 tablespoons mayonnaise

1 tablespoon prepared yellow mustard

2 teaspoons Chesapeake Bay seasoning

2 pounds crabmeat, backfin or special preferred, picked over for shells and cartilage

8 slices white bread, crusts removed and bread cubed

¼ cup (½ stick) unsalted butter, melted

Crab loaves are party stars all along the Chesapeake Bay. "Loaf" is sort of a misnomer because these are actually little baked squares. Mrs. Frances Kitching of Smith Island Boarding House fame is credited with developing this little munchie, although there are plenty of cooks in the region who disagree about its origin. **SERVES 10 TO 12**

1. Preheat the oven to 350°F. Lightly butter a 10 x 14-inch baking dish.

2. Melt the 3 tablespoons butter in a medium-size skillet over medium heat. Add the onion and bell pepper and cook, stirring, until slightly soft and translucent, about 5 minutes. Set aside.

3. Whisk the cornstarch and milk together in a small saucepan until the cornstarch has dissolved. Continue to whisk over low heat until a smooth paste forms. (This step is to cook out the starch taste in the cornstarch.) Remove from the heat.

4. In a medium-size mixing bowl, combine the eggs, mayonnaise, mustard, Bay seasoning, and cornstarch mixture. Add the sautéed onion and bell pepper and mix well. Add the crabmeat and half of the bread cubes and mix gently.

5. Transfer the crab mixture to the prepared dish and spread evenly without packing it down. Arrange the remaining bread cubes evenly on top. Spoon the melted butter over the cubes. Bake until hot and browned, about 35 minutes.

6. Remove the pan from the oven and let stand for 5 minutes. Cut into 3-inch squares and serve hot.

crab cheesecake

In 1985, this cheesecake by Phyllis Murphy won the grand prize in a crab cooking contest in Crisfield, Maryland, at the National Hard Crab Derby & Fair. I've tried seafood cheesecakes by some of the great chefs, and I still think this one is the best. Not only can you serve this cold with crackers as part of a cocktail buffet, but you also can serve slices of it warm as a first course or even for brunch. **SERVES 12 FOR A COCKTAIL PARTY OR 6 AS A FIRST COURSE**

1. To make the crust, preheat the oven to 350°F. Combine the crackers and butter, then press the mixture evenly over the bottom of a 9-inch springform pan. Bake for 10 minutes, then set aside to cool. Reduce the oven temperature to 325°F.

2. To make the filling, in a large mixing bowl with an electric mixer, beat the cream cheese, eggs, and sour cream together until fluffy. Add the lemon juice, onion, Bay seasoning, Tabasco, and pepper and beat to combine. Stir in the crabmeat until well mixed. Pour into the cooled crust and smooth the top with a rubber spatula. Bake until the cake is set, about 50 minutes.

3. Remove from the oven. Run a knife around the edge of the cake, loosening it from the sides of the pan. Let cool for 30 minutes on a wire rack.

4. Remove the sides of the pan and top with the sour cream.

Crust:

1 cup roughly crushed butter crackers (such as Ritz)

3 tablespoons unsalted butter, melted

Filling:

Two 8-ounce packages cream cheese, softened

3 medium-size eggs

¼ cup sour cream

1 teaspoon fresh lemon juice

2 teaspoons grated yellow onion

½ teaspoon Chesapeake Bay seasoning

1 drop Tabasco sauce

⅛ teaspoon freshly ground black pepper

½ pound crabmeat, picked over for shells and cartilage

Topping:

½ cup sour cream

Dungeness crab spring rolls with cilantro-Garlic Dipping sauce

½ pound ground pork

1 tablespoon peanut oil

¼ teaspoon toasted sesame oil

1 tablespoon peeled and finely minced fresh ginger

2 cloves garlic, minced

1 tablespoon fermented black beans in garlic sauce, chopped

1 tablespoon hot pepper sauce

½ pound Dungeness crabmeat, picked over for shells and cartilage

3 scallions (white and green parts), finely chopped

¼ cup chopped fresh cilantro leaves

6 sheets frozen phyllo dough, defrosted

¼ cup olive oil

1 large egg white

Cilantro-Garlic Dipping Sauce (recipe follows)

asians have long known how well pork and crab blend together, and this recipe takes advantage of that pairing. Calling these spring rolls is a bit of menu speak, because I've taken a shortcut and used phyllo dough and baked them in long rolls, almost like a strudel. The rolls come together quickly and can be made in advance, then baked at the last minute. Not only are they a superlative first course, but when sliced into smaller pieces, they make a great finger food for a cocktail party. Fermented black beans, or Chinese black beans, are black soybeans that have been preserved with salt. You'll find them in most supermarkets in the Asian foods section, usually packed in jars with oil. They are very pungent and, of course, salty. You can leave them out for a tamer dish. **SERVES 6 AS A FIRST COURSE**

1. Heat a skillet over medium-high heat. Add the pork, peanut oil, and sesame oil and cook, stirring often, until the pork is cooked through. Stir in the ginger, garlic, beans, and hot pepper sauce. Remove the skillet from the heat and stir in the crab, scallions, and cilantro. Set aside to cool.

2. Preheat the oven to 350°F.

3. Remove the phyllo dough from the package and cover with a damp cloth to prevent it from drying out. Whisk together the olive oil and egg white. To make the rolls, separate 1 sheet of phyllo. Brush it lightly with the olive oil mixture. Top with a second sheet of phyllo and brush with the mixture. Top with another sheet of phyllo and brush again with the mixture. With the longer edge of the sheet facing you, spread half of the crab mixture across the bottom edge of the dough, leaving a 1-inch border on

the bottom and at the sides. Roll the sheet up tightly to create a long, thin roll about 1½ inches in diameter. Tuck the ends of the sheet under the roll. Place on an ungreased baking sheet and brush with the olive oil mixture. Repeat with the remaining phyllo and filling to form another roll and place on the baking sheet.

4. Bake the rolls until crisp and golden, 12 to 15 minutes. Let rest for 5 minutes before slicing each roll into 6 pieces, using a serrated knife. Serve 2 pieces per person, with a little ramekin of the dipping sauce on the side.

cilantro-garlic dipping sauce

This inviting dipping sauce is also good with steamed dumplings or cold cracked crab. **MAKES ABOUT ½ CUP**

Whisk everything together in a small mixing bowl. Let sit at room temperature for about 30 minutes to allow the flavors to meld before serving.

⅓ cup tamari or other low-sodium soy sauce

2 tablespoons unseasoned rice vinegar

⅛ teaspoon toasted sesame oil

2 cloves garlic, minced

¼ teaspoon peeled and finely minced fresh ginger

1 tablespoon chopped fresh cilantro leaves

CRAB-FILLED POT STICKERS WITH HONEY-GINGER DIPPING SAUCE

Honey-ginger dipping sauce:

2 tablespoons tamari or other low-sodium soy sauce

1 tablespoon honey

1½ teaspoons Dijon mustard

1 tablespoon water

1 teaspoon unseasoned rice vinegar

½ teaspoon peeled and finely minced fresh ginger

¼ teaspoon toasted sesame oil

1 teaspoon chopped fresh chives

Pot stickers:

2 scallions (white and green parts), chopped

2 tablespoons sesame seeds, toasted (see Note)

2 large egg whites

2½ teaspoons peeled and finely minced fresh ginger

1 pound crabmeat, lump blue or Dungeness preferred, picked over for shells and cartilage

24 wonton wrappers

2 tablespoons cornstarch

2 to 3 tablespoons canola oil

½ cup water

Pot stickers are just plain fun to eat. Many of us reserve these treats for a night at an Asian restaurant, but they are easy to make at home. Using wonton wrappers, either fresh or frozen, cuts way down on the hassle. Anything can become a pot sticker; this recipe is just a good place to start. Try adding chopped cooked shrimp, or go really upscale and mix the crabmeat with some finely minced duck confit. The dipping sauce is a variation on the most common dipping sauce for pot stickers, but these also are good with crab Louis dressing (see page 112). You can make them in advance up to the cooking stage and refrigerate for 1 day or freeze for 1 week. Wonton wrappers and toasted sesame oil can be found in Asian markets and some large supermarkets. **SERVES 4**

1. To make the dipping sauce, combine all the ingredients in a small bowl and set aside.

2. To make the pot stickers, combine the scallions, sesame seeds, egg whites, and ginger in a large mixing bowl. Gently fold in the crabmeat, taking care to keep the lumps as big as possible.

3. Place 12 of the wonton wrappers on a dry counter. Brush the edges with water. Place 1 tablespoon of the crab mixture in the center of each wrapper. Pull each wrapper up around the filling, crimping the dough, but do not cover the top; the filling should come to the top of the wrapper. Sprinkle the cornstarch on a plate and set each pot sticker in the cornstarch. Repeat with the remaining 12 wrappers.

4. Heat the canola oil in a large nonstick skillet over medium-high heat until it shimmers but hasn't started to smoke. Working in batches to avoid crowding, place the pot stickers cornstarch side down in the skillet and fry until golden brown, which will take only about 1 minute. Carefully add the water down the side of the pan, cover, reduce the heat to low, and steam for about 2 minutes. Uncover and continue to cook until the water has evaporated.

5. Place 6 pot stickers on each serving plate and serve with the dipping sauce.

Note: Don't bother to defrost frozen pot stickers before cooking them. Simply add a bit more water and a few extra minutes to the steaming time.

   To toast sesame seeds, place them in a dry small skillet over medium heat and toast until fragrant and lightly browned.

miniature crab cakes with tomato-ginger jam

½ cup mayonnaise

1 large egg

1 tablespoon Dijon mustard

1 teaspoon Chesapeake Bay seasoning

1½ teaspoons fresh lemon juice

¼ teaspoon kosher salt

⅛ teaspoon freshly ground black pepper

⅛ teaspoon hot pepper sauce

1 pound crabmeat, jumbo lump backfin preferred, picked over for shells and cartilage

2 cups corn flake crumbs

2 cups panko (Japanese bread crumbs)

Tomato-Ginger Jam (recipe follows)

Roughly chopped fresh Italian parsley leaves for garnish

I really like this recipe for a party because the cakes are baked—no fried smell to turn off your guests. Plus, you can prepare them ahead and bake them as needed to replenish your cocktail buffet. Finally, they can always be made into full-size portions for a light dinner or luncheon. I use a combination of corn flake crumbs and Japanese bread crumbs, called panko, to coat these cakes. The mix gives them a sweet note and great texture, but you could use all of one or the other. **MAKES ABOUT 36 HORS D'OEUVRE–SIZE CAKES; SERVES 12**

1. Whisk together the mayonnaise, egg, mustard, Bay seasoning, lemon juice, salt, black pepper, and hot pepper sauce in a large mixing bowl. Gently stir in the crabmeat, taking care not to break up the lumps. Cover with plastic wrap and refrigerate for at least 2 hours but not much more.

2. Combine the corn flake crumbs and panko in a shallow dish. Set aside.

3. Form heaping teaspoons of the crab mixture into 1½-inch-diameter cakes (the mixture will be very moist). Place on a greased baking sheet, cover with plastic wrap, and refrigerate for at least 30 minutes or up to 3 hours.

4. Gently dredge the cakes with the corn flake–panko mixture, tapping off any excess. Return to the refrigerator for up to 3 hours.

5. Preheat the oven to 400°F.

6. Bake the crab cakes as you need them in the center of the oven until crisp and golden, 8 to 10 minutes. Transfer with a metal spatula to a platter and top each with a bit of jam and a sprinkle of parsley. Serve hot or at room temperature.

TOMATO-GINGER JAM

The combination of tomato and ginger was meant for seafood. Joe, the seafood manager at Citarella, a gourmet food shop in New York City, first suggested that I pick up a jar of tomato-ginger chutney to go with a piece of halibut, and from that point on, I kept trying it with all kinds of fish and shellfish. After searching for a good recipe for homemade chutney, I settled on this quick jam that I got from my neighbor Verla Gabrial, which delights the tongue and marries perfectly with these crab cakes. Don't hesitate to use the jam with other recipes in this book or even fish dishes that you might create. **MAKES ABOUT 2 CUPS**

2 tablespoons unsalted butter

¼ cup minced shallots

1 tablespoon peeled and finely minced fresh ginger

1 large clove garlic, minced

¾ teaspoon kosher salt

¼ teaspoon freshly ground black pepper

⅛ teaspoon red pepper flakes

1 tablespoon sugar

1½ pounds ripe plum tomatoes, seeded and finely chopped

1½ tablespoons fresh lime juice

2 tablespoons finely chopped fresh cilantro leaves

1. Melt the butter in a 10-inch heavy skillet over medium-low heat. Add the shallots, ginger, garlic, salt, black pepper, and red pepper flakes and cook, stirring, until the shallots are softened, about 5 minutes. Add the sugar and cook, stirring, until dissolved. Add the tomatoes and simmer over medium heat, stirring occasionally, until thickened, 10 to 15 minutes.

2. Remove from the heat and let cool to room temperature. The jam can be made up to 2 days ahead, covered, and stored in the refrigerator. Stir in the lime juice and cilantro right before serving.

¼ cup (½ stick) unsalted butter, melted

½ teaspoon kosher salt

1 teaspoon Chesapeake Bay seasoning

1 teaspoon dry mustard

½ teaspoon hot pepper sauce

½ cup roughly crushed saltines

1 pound crabmeat, picked over for shells and cartilage

2 large egg yolks, lightly beaten

Peanut or canola oil for frying

All-purpose flour for dredging

Crab critters could just as easily be called crab balls. They are a variation of a miniature crab cake. Don't try to shape them too much; let them be sort of wild. The trick is not to fry them too long; just let them get golden brown and heated through. Even though I first learned of these in Crisfield, Maryland, I like to serve them with the West Coast standard, crab Louis dressing (see page 112). They also are pretty good with the anchovy dressing I use with the cobb salad on page 90. **MAKES 24 TO 48 CRAB BALLS, DEPENDING ON THE SIZE; SERVES 12 TO 16**

1. Combine the butter, salt, Bay seasoning, mustard, hot pepper sauce, and saltines in a medium-size bowl and mix well. Stir in the crabmeat and beaten egg yolks. Cover with plastic wrap and refrigerate until firm, about 1 hour.

2. Heat 3 inches of oil in a deep skillet or deep fryer to 365°F.

3. Meanwhile, using a teaspoon as a guide, roll the mixture into small balls and dredge with flour, tapping off any excess. Fry the balls in the hot oil, taking care not to crowd them, until they are a nice golden brown, 3 to 5 minutes. Drain on paper towels or brown paper bags. (Draining on bags will give you a crisper crust.) Serve at once.

spicy crab claws

To me, no crab claw preparation will ever top plain old crab claws and cocktail sauce, but this recipe is an interesting and tasty twist. Folks in Florida, especially in the Keys, lay claim to this concoction, but I found variations along the Eastern Shore and even in California. These claws are a little messy to eat, so be sure to have some extra napkins around.

SERVES 24

1. Combine all the ingredients except the crab claws in a medium-size saucepan and cook over low heat for 10 minutes.

2. Place the crab claws in a zippered-top plastic bag or glass baking dish and pour the marinade over them. Zip closed or cover with plastic wrap and refrigerate for several hours.

3. At serving time, drain the marinade, arrange the claws on a platter, and serve with crackers or party bread.

Note: Dungeness crab claws also work well in this recipe.

½ cup minced scallions (white and green parts)

2 cloves garlic, finely minced

1 cup olive oil

½ teaspoon kosher salt

½ teaspoon freshly ground black pepper

½ cup red wine vinegar

½ cup chopped fresh Italian parsley leaves

3 tablespoons fresh lemon juice

1 tablespoon Worcestershire sauce

½ teaspoon hot pepper sauce

2 to 3 pounds blue crab cocktail claws

WONDERFUL SOUPS

For most of America, the gold standard of crab soups is she-crab soup. The romance of Charleston, South Carolina, and the low country, matched with the silken richness and hints of sherry, has made she-crab soup, according to some, "the New England clam chowder of the South."

But she-crab is just one of many mighty fine illustrations of what happens when crab hits the soup pot. Take a look at any Southern community cookbook and you will see how busy folks have been using crab in soup. Cream of mushroom, shrimp, or asparagus soup with some crabmeat stirred in right before serving is considered an elegant first course by many, and rightfully so.

The examples in this chapter will take you from the simple to the exotic, with interesting regional variations along the way. There is one very important caveat: add the crabmeat where it is called for in the recipes, which, in many cases, is just before serving. This allows the full flavor of the crabmeat to contrast with the other ingredients. I also recommend that you consider all claw meat in soups, unless you find the reddish color to be out of character with the occasion. Claw meat is much cheaper than other grades and has a bolder crab essence.

apple-coconut crab chowder

2 tablespoons unsalted butter

2 cups finely chopped yellow onion

3 Granny Smith apples

2 tablespoons fresh lemon juice

4 medium-size kaffir lime leaves or grated zest of 1 lime

2 ½ cups reduced-sodium chicken broth

1 cup water

½ cup canned unsweetened coconut milk

1 tablespoon sugar

Kosher salt and white pepper to taste

1 pound crabmeat, picked over for shells and cartilage

Grated lime zest for garnish

Inspired by a soup from award-winning cookbook author Nicole Routhier, this soup is a blend of common and exotic ingredients just waiting to tease your tongue. Kaffir lime leaves are the mystery flavor. Once found only in Thai groceries, kaffir lime leaves have become more commonplace and can now be found at natural food stores and in the produce department of larger supermarkets. Canned unsweetened coconut milk is available in the Asian foods section of most supermarkets. Lump Dungeness or blue crab meat works best in this recipe. If you have access to Jonah crab claw meat, by all means try it. **SERVES 4 TO 6 AS A LIGHT LUNCH OR FIRST COURSE**

1. Melt the butter in a 3-quart or larger saucepan over medium-low heat. When it stops foaming, add the onion and cook, stirring occasionally, until soft but not colored, 5 to 6 minutes.

2. While the onion is cooking, peel and core the apples, then slice into eighths. Sprinkle with the lemon juice. Add the apples and lime leaves to the onion, cover, and cook, stirring occasionally, until the apples are slightly mushy, about 10 minutes. Add the chicken broth, water, coconut milk, and sugar and bring to a boil. Reduce the heat to low and simmer for 10 minutes. Season with salt and white pepper.

3. Remove the lime leaves. Puree the soup in batches in a blender or food processor, or puree it in the pan with a hand-held immersion blender. Bring the soup back to a simmer.

4. Divide the crabmeat evenly among the soup bowls. Ladle the hot soup over the crabmeat and garnish with lime zest.

CHRISSY'S CRAB CHOWDER

With this chowder recipe, Christine Dryden won first place in the soup division of the 2001 Crisfield, Maryland, National Hard Crab Derby & Fair Cooking Contest. I wholeheartedly agree with the judges' decision. Christine and her mom, Jo, have been competing together and winning in almost every category for more than 13 years. Lately, Christine's dad, Lit, has gotten into the fray and has brought home a prize as well. When you talk with these folks, well, they can make you smile in about 10 seconds, and cooking together is just a fun part of their lives.

What I like about this chowder is how simple it is, yet it is a perfect example of a quintessential chowder—each component is independent but married to the whole. **SERVES 4 TO 6**

Melt the butter in a medium-size soup pot over medium heat. Add the onion and celery and cook, stirring, until translucent, about 2 minutes. Reduce the heat to low, add the flour, and mix well until pasty. Using a whisk and stirring slowly, add the bacon, potatoes, parsley, paprika, garlic salt, celery salt, white pepper, Bay seasoning, and salt and black pepper. Slowly add the milk and cream, stirring constantly. Add the corn, then gently fold in the crabmeat. Cook until just heated through. Serve hot.

½ cup (1 stick) unsalted butter

1 medium-size yellow onion, diced

2 stalks celery, diced

¾ cup all-purpose flour

10 strips bacon, chopped and cooked just until it begins to render its fat and brown; it should still be soft

5 medium-size Yukon Gold potatoes, peeled, diced, parboiled for about 5 minutes, and drained

¼ cup chopped fresh Italian parsley leaves

¼ teaspoon paprika

⅛ teaspoon garlic salt

⅛ teaspoon celery salt

⅛ teaspoon white pepper

1 teaspoon Chesapeake Bay seasoning

Kosher salt and freshly ground black pepper to taste

1 quart whole milk

2 cups heavy cream

One 14-ounce can corn kernels, drained

1 pound Maryland blue crabmeat, claw meat preferred, picked over for shells and cartilage

FISH, SHRIMP, AND CRAB CHOWDER

3 tablespoons unsalted butter

2 cups finely chopped yellow onion

2 cups bottled clam juice

2 cups reduced-sodium chicken broth

1 bay leaf

¾ teaspoon kosher salt

½ teaspoon freshly ground black pepper

4 cups peeled and diced all-purpose potatoes

¾ cup milk

1 cup heavy cream

½ pound firm, white-fleshed fish fillets (such as cod, scrod, haddock, hake, monkfish, halibut, or grouper), cut into bite-size chunks

½ pound medium-size shrimp, peeled, deveined, and halved

½ cup minced fresh Italian parsley leaves

½ pound crabmeat, lump preferred, picked over for shells and cartilage

One of my favorite seafood chowders comes from Anna Pump's *Loaves and Fishes Cookbook*. Pump built a solid reputation for exceptional food at her East Hampton, Long Island, gourmet shop. This easy-to-make but oh-so-good chowder keeps my soup pot busy during the fall and winter. Not one to leave well enough alone, I've tinkered with the recipe a bit and found that adding crabmeat just plain puts it over the top. This chowder also tastes every bit as good the next day. **SERVES 6**

1. Melt the butter in a large soup pot over medium-high heat. When it stops foaming, add the onion and cook, stirring, until soft and transparent, about 5 minutes. Add the clam juice, chicken broth, bay leaf, salt, pepper, and potatoes and bring to a boil. Reduce the heat to low and simmer for 20 minutes.

2. Pour in the milk and cream and bring back to a boil. Add the fish chunks and bring back to a boil. Stir in the shrimp. Reduce the heat to medium and simmer for 3 minutes. Stir in the parsley and crabmeat and just heat through, about 1 minute. Serve immediately.

corn and crab chowder

Summer gives a bounty of flavorful gems. One of the greatest pairings is field-fresh corn and the sweet meat of the blue crab. Instead of salt pork, I start with bacon, because I like the added smokiness. "Rhode Island style" might describe the texture, letting the ingredients shine instead of the starch. The use of canned corn is a shortcut for a tasty broth that I think you will like. **SERVES 6 TO 8**

1. Place the bacon in a 5-quart soup pot and cook over medium heat, stirring, until the fat is rendered and the bacon is crisp. Use a slotted spoon to transfer the bacon to paper towels to drain.

2. Add the onion and butter to the bacon grease and cook slowly, stirring a few times, until translucent, 5 to 7 minutes. Stir in the flour and cook for 5 minutes. Stirring, add the chicken broth, then the Bay seasoning and oregano. Bring to a boil, reduce the heat to medium-low, and simmer for 10 minutes. Pour in the creamed corn and cook for 10 minutes. Add the potatoes and cook for 10 minutes. Stir in the fresh corn and crabmeat and cook for 5 minutes. Add the cream and heat the soup to a simmer. Continue to simmer for 5 minutes; *do not allow it to come to a boil.*

3. Serve in warmed soup bowls, garnished with the chives and reserved bacon.

Variation: To intensify the corn flavor, add the corncobs when you add the chicken broth. Remove them before you add the creamed corn.

Note: To make ahead, prepare through step 2 and refrigerate. When ready to serve, bring the soup to a simmer and continue as directed.

4 strips thick-cut apple wood– or hickory-smoked bacon, diced

1 cup finely chopped yellow onion

1 tablespoon unsalted butter

2 tablespoons gravy flour (such as Wondra)

6 cups reduced-sodium chicken broth

1 teaspoon Chesapeake Bay seasoning

¼ teaspoon dried oregano

One 14.5-ounce can creamed corn

3 cups peeled and diced russet potatoes

4 cups fresh corn kernels

1 pound crabmeat, claw meat preferred, picked over for shells and cartilage

1 cup heavy cream or half-and-half

¼ cup chopped fresh chives

HOT-aND-SOUr SOUP WITH Crab

3 dried Chinese black mushrooms

1 ounce dried shiitake mushrooms

6 cups reduced-sodium chicken broth

3 tablespoons peeled fresh ginger cut into matchsticks

1 teaspoon chopped garlic

2 teaspoons Chinese chili paste with garlic

¼ cup tamari or other low-sodium soy sauce

1 cup canned sliced bamboo shoots, drained

1 tablespoon fresh lime juice

2 teaspoons sugar

Kosher salt to taste

1 tablespoon plus 2 teaspoons cornstarch

2 tablespoons cold water

1 large egg, lightly beaten

¼ cup unseasoned rice vinegar or 3 tablespoons cider vinegar (see Note)

1 cup crabmeat, picked over for shells and cartilage

¼ cup chopped scallions (white and green parts)

With a fiery mix of chili paste and vinegar, hot-and-sour soup has become a popular starter at American Chinese restaurants. This soup is usually made with pork, but crab is an elegant substitute that plays well with the traditional flavors. Dungeness crab is a favorite of Asians, but lump blue crab works just as well. If you need a cure for a nasty head cold, ladle up a bowl of this elixir and enjoy your medicine. **SERVES 4**

1. Place the dried mushrooms in a small heatproof bowl and cover with boiling water. Let soak for 30 minutes. Drain, rinse, and pat dry, then cut into thin slices. Set aside.

2. In a 3-quart saucepan, bring the chicken broth to a boil. Reduce the heat to medium-low. Add the ginger, garlic, chili paste, tamari, sliced mushrooms, and bamboo shoots and simmer for 10 minutes. Stir in the lime juice and sugar. Season with salt.

3. Make a slurry by mixing together the cornstarch and water. Add the slurry to the soup, slowly bring to a boil, and cook for a few minutes at a boil until the soup thickens.

4. Slowly pour the beaten egg into the soup, stirring gently a few times with a spoon or chopsticks. You are trying to get the egg to form shreds. Don't stir too fast, or the effect will be lost. The egg will cook almost instantly. Remove the soup from the heat and stir in the vinegar.

5. To serve, divide the crabmeat among 4 bowls. Ladle the hot soup over the crabmeat, garnish with the scallions, and serve immediately.

Note: If vinegar is not your favorite taste, add it in step 2 with the other ingredients. You will still get a sour component, but it will be much milder.

california cioppino

2 precooked Dungeness crabs (1½ to 2 pounds each)

24 Manila clams, well scrubbed

3 cups dry white wine

⅓ cup olive oil

1 medium-size yellow onion, finely chopped

3 large cloves garlic, minced

1 medium-size green bell pepper, seeded and coarsely chopped

2 pounds ripe tomatoes, peeled, seeded, and chopped

2 tablespoons tomato paste

1 teaspoon Worcestershire sauce

1 teaspoon freshly ground black pepper

½ teaspoon dried oregano

1 tablespoon finely chopped fresh basil leaves or ½ teaspoon dried

2 pounds firm, white-fleshed fish fillets (such as sea bass, cod, or halibut), cut into 1-inch pieces

¾ pound sea scallops

¾ pound medium-size shrimp, peeled and deveined

Chopped fresh Italian parsley leaves

I thank the Italian immigrants of San Francisco for the pleasure I get every time I make cioppino, which is often. Based loosely on the Mediterranean fish soup bouillabaisse, cioppino is much less complicated to make. There are many variations on cioppino—probably as many as there are Italian grandmothers. This recipe captures the idea of a seafood-packed, tomato-based meal in a single pot. Cioppino is made for entertaining; it is easy to make the broth ahead, then cook the seafood at the last minute. Serve with copious amounts of crusty sourdough bread to sop up the last of the broth and a simple green salad for a yummy dinner party. **SERVES 8**

1. Remove the legs and claws from the crab and break the body in half, reserving as much of the soft, mustard-colored fat as possible. Set the crab pieces aside.

2. Place the clams in a medium-size saucepan, add 1 cup of the wine, and steam, covered, over medium heat until the clams open, 4 to 6 minutes. Remove the clams from the saucepan, discarding any that do not open, and set aside. Reserve the cooking liquid.

3. Heat the oil in an 8-quart soup pot over medium heat. Add the onion, garlic, and bell pepper and cook, stirring a few times, until the vegetables start to soften, about 5 minutes. Add the tomatoes, tomato paste, Worcestershire, remaining 2 cups wine, black pepper, oregano, basil, and reserved cooking liquid. Partially cover and simmer for 20 minutes.

4. Add the fish, scallops, shrimp, crab pieces, and crab fat. Simmer until all the seafood is cooked through, about 5 minutes. Do not stir. Add the clams and just heat through. Sprinkle with parsley and serve immediately in big bowls with lots of napkins.

If folks in Baltimore and the upper Eastern Shore will forgive me, I'd like to rename this soup Chesapeake Bay stew because of its thick, need-to-use-a-fork-to-eat-it heartiness. Almost every restaurant I visited in the area had a variation of this soup, sometimes calling it Maryland crab soup or vegetable crab soup. The really good ones reminded me of the Brunswick stews I grew up on in North Carolina. As the cold fall breezes start blowing across the bay, I can't think of a better dish to fortify the body and soul.

SERVES 10 TO 12

1. Heat the oil in a 5-quart or larger soup pot over medium-high heat. Cut the meat off the beef shin into cubes. Add the beef cubes and shin to the hot oil and brown on all sides. Stir in the onion and cook, stirring a few times, until limp, 5 to 6 minutes. Add the celery and cook, stirring, until soft, about 5 minutes. Add the water, crabs, crushed tomatoes, diced tomatoes, and tomato paste and stir to combine. Add the ham hock, bouillon, bay leaf, Bay seasoning, and parsley and stir to blend. Bring to a boil, reduce the heat to a low simmer, and cook for 1 hour.

2. Remove the ham hock, let cool slightly, and pick the meat out of it. Return the meat to the pot. Remove the crabs and bay leaf. Pick the crabs for the meat and set the meat aside. Add the cabbage, potatoes, and mixed vegetables to the pot and cook, stirring occasionally, for 1 hour.

3. Stir the meat from the picked crabs and the 2 pounds crabmeat into the soup and heat through, about 10 minutes. Serve hot.

1 tablespoon olive oil

¾ pound bone-in beef shin

2 cups chopped yellow onion

¼ cup chopped celery

6 cups water

4 live blue crabs, steamed (see page 118)

One 28-ounce can crushed tomatoes, undrained

One 14.5-ounce can diced tomatoes, undrained

One 6-ounce can tomato paste

1 small smoked ham hock

2 beef bouillon cubes

1 bay leaf

1 tablespoon Chesapeake Bay seasoning

¼ cup chopped fresh Italian parsley leaves

4 cups cored and roughly chopped cabbage

1 pound white or Yukon Gold potatoes, peeled and cut into ½-inch dice

Two 10-ounce boxes frozen mixed vegetables

2 pounds crabmeat, claw meat preferred, picked over for shells and cartilage

Bessie's Seafood Bisque

½ pound shrimp, peeled, deveined, and chopped

½ pint shucked small oysters, with their liquor

1 cup water

½ pound crabmeat, picked over for shells and cartilage

4 cups reduced-sodium chicken broth

1 cup heavy cream

1 cup milk

2 tablespoons unsalted butter

¼ teaspoon Worcestershire sauce

⅛ teaspoon white pepper

⅛ teaspoon freshly grated nutmeg

Cream sherry for sprinkling (optional)

Paprika for sprinkling

Mrs. Bessie Gibbs had quite the reputation as a cook in her day. As the owner, with her husband, Gibby, of the Island Hotel in Cedar Key, Florida, she is credited with creating the hearts of palm salad famous in south Florida, over-the-top spoon bread, and this bisque. It is a simple, quick, and appetizing soup. My in-laws, Sam and B. A. Schlegel, longtime Florida residents, introduced me to Mrs. Gibbs's cooking and keep me current regarding all manner of Florida cuisine. The Gibbses are gone, but the hotel is still operating as a wonderful inn. **SERVES 4 TO 6**

1. Place the shrimp and oysters in a 3-quart saucepan and add the water. Bring to a boil, then reduce the heat to a simmer. Add the crabmeat, chicken broth, cream, milk, butter, Worcestershire, white pepper, and nutmeg and simmer until hot. *Do not allow it to come to a boil.*

2. Divide the soup among soup bowls. Sprinkle with a little cream sherry, if using, and paprika before serving.

pumpkin crab soup

Since blue crab season extends through October and Dungeness crab season starts rolling in November, mixing crabmeat with another fall favorite—pumpkin—is a no-brainer. I wanted a light finish to this soup, so I used the old method of thickening soup with bread. With just a little bit of cream added at the end, this interesting fall soup becomes rich and satisfying, without having all the calories provided by a cream base or roux. All claw meat is the best choice for this seasonal treat. You can substitute any fall squash for the pumpkin with great success. **SERVES 8 AS A FIRST COURSE OR 4 AS A MAIN COURSE**

1. If using fresh pumpkin, place in a medium-size saucepan and cover with water. Bring to a boil, reduce the heat to a simmer, and cook until tender, about 30 minutes. Drain.

2. Combine the pumpkin, apples, chicken broth, water, bread, onion, rosemary, marjoram, and pepper in a large soup pot and bring to a boil. Reduce the heat to medium-low and simmer, uncovered, for 45 minutes.

3. In a food processor or blender, process the soup until smooth. Or puree it in the pot with a hand-held immersion blender. Reheat the soup, then stir in the cream and crabmeat and heat through.

4. Serve immediately, garnished with the parsley.

1 pound peeled and seeded pumpkin (1 small pumpkin) or one 16-ounce can pumpkin puree

3 Granny Smith apples, peeled, cored, and chopped

3 cups reduced-sodium chicken broth

1½ cups water

3 slices white bread, torn into pieces

½ cup chopped yellow onion

¼ teaspoon dried rosemary

¼ teaspoon dried marjoram

¼ teaspoon freshly ground black pepper

¼ cup heavy cream

1 pound crabmeat, claw meat preferred, picked over for shells and cartilage

¼ cup chopped fresh Italian parsley leaves for garnish

sHe-craB soup

She-crab soup is the classic of all crab soups. What would a trip to Charleston, South Carolina, or anywhere in the low country be without a bowl of sherry-infused she-crab soup? This cream-based soup is ideally flavored with crab roe, which also imparts a wonderful texture. However, unless you are willing to steam your own blue she-crabs, called sooks, during the spring when they are full of pungent roe, you won't be able to savor the authentic flavor of this soup. Sometimes you can find frozen roe, but I've also found that crabmeat processed in the Gulf coast region has a high percentage of roe included with the meat. Ask your fishmonger for a container of crabmeat with a good amount of roe. An acceptable substitute for the richness and texture of she-crab roe is a hard-boiled egg yolk. Heck, even with an abundant amount of roe, I like egg yolks in my she-crab soup. This recipe is for a basic she-crab soup. The one that follows takes on a more pronounced low country twist. **SERVES 8**

½ cup (1 stick) unsalted butter

1 large yellow onion, finely diced

1 cup all-purpose flour

5 cups half-and-half

2 cups heavy cream

½ teaspoon ground mace

½ cup good-quality dry sherry

Kosher salt and freshly ground black pepper to taste

½ pound crabmeat with lots of roe, picked over for shells and cartilage, or (better yet) 6 to 8 sooks, boiled or steamed (see page 117 or 118) and picked of their meat and roe (see page 28)

2 hard-boiled large egg yolks, pushed through a sieve

1. Melt the butter in a large soup pot over medium heat. When it stops foaming, add the onion and cook, stirring a few times, until softened and translucent, about 5 minutes. Add the flour, reduce the heat to low, and stir constantly for about 5 minutes. Add the half-and-half and cream, whisking constantly, and continue to whisk until slightly thickened and smooth. Add the mace and sherry and simmer for 30 minutes, stirring frequently. Season with salt and black pepper.

2. When ready to serve, stir in the crabmeat and roe (if you are so fortunate) and the egg yolks. Serve immediately.

pawleys island she-crab soup

¼ cup (½ stick) unsalted butter

1 cup finely chopped yellow onion

½ cup finely chopped celery

1 cup finely chopped leeks
(white part only)

1 bay leaf

⅛ teaspoon dried thyme

⅛ teaspoon cayenne pepper

2 teaspoons kosher salt

½ cup converted long-grain
white rice

3 cups bottled clam juice

2 cups water

2 cups heavy cream

1 pound crabmeat, lump
preferred, picked over for
shells or cartilage, or 6 to 8
sooks, boiled or steamed
(see page 117 or 118) and
picked of their meat and roe
(see page 28)

6 tablespoons amontillado sherry,
or to taste

½ teaspoon fresh lemon juice
(optional)

½ cup crab roe (not needed if you
cooked your own sooks), finely
chopped

1 tablespoon finely chopped
fresh Italian parsley leaves for
garnish (optional)

1 tablespoon finely chopped fresh
tarragon leaves for garnish
(optional)

In this more elaborate version of she-crab soup, rice is used as a thickening agent. Author John Martin Taylor of Charleston, South Carolina, has long been a proponent of this method. The rice banner has been picked up and carried by such great Southern chefs as Louis Osteen, who makes a killer she-crab soup at his restaurant on Pawleys Island, South Carolina. This recipe was inspired by Chef Osteen. **SERVES 8**

1. Melt the butter in a large, heavy soup pot over medium heat. When it stops foaming, add the onion, celery, and leeks and cook, stirring occasionally, until soft and translucent, about 10 minutes. Add the bay leaf, thyme, cayenne, salt, rice, clam juice, and water. Bring to a simmer, reduce the heat to low, and simmer for 30 minutes, stirring every now and then.

2. Increase the heat to medium-high, add the cream, and bring to a boil. Reduce the heat to medium (make sure the cream does not bubble up) and simmer for 5 minutes, stirring occasionally.

3. Remove from the heat and let cool for 10 minutes. Remove the bay leaf, then puree the soup in a blender, food processor, or food mill. Or puree it in the pot using a hand-held immersion blender. For a very smooth soup, strain it, pushing down on the solids to get as much flavor as possible. Return the soup to the pot.

4. Place the pot over medium heat and add the crabmeat. Bring to a boil, stirring. Stir in the sherry. You might want to add half the sherry, then taste and flavor to your liking. Add the lemon juice, if you wish. Add the roe, if using, and warm for a minute or two.

5. Serve in bowls, garnished with parsley and tarragon, if desired.

sam miller's warehouse crab soup

On a weekend trip to Richmond, Virginia, I wanted to check out a hot new restaurant called the Tobacco Company in the Shockoe Slip area near the James River. The wait for a table was over an hour, and, not one who has ever been fond of waiting, I looked for plan B. To this day, I'm glad that the Tobacco Company was so busy. Across the street was (and still is) Sam Miller's Warehouse and one of the best crab soups I have ever eaten. Years later, I acquired the recipe for the soup, and I've been a happy boy ever since. This is a roux-based cream soup and is not as thick as many restaurants tend to make such soups, letting the crab flavor take center stage. Substitute clams for the crab, add a couple of diced potatoes, and you have a superb New England–style chowder. **SERVES 8**

Melt the butter in a large soup pot over medium heat. When it stops foaming, add the onion and cook, stirring a few times, until soft and translucent, about 5 minutes. Stirring constantly, add the flour and cook until a smooth golden paste forms. Add the milk and half-and-half all at once, then stir in the chicken bouillon, thyme, and white pepper. Stir constantly until the soup has thickened and is smooth, about 5 minutes. Stir in the sherry and crabmeat and heat through. Serve immediately.

¼ cup (½ stick) unsalted butter

1 small yellow onion, finely chopped

⅓ cup all-purpose flour, or more as needed to thicken

2 quarts milk, heated

2 cups half-and-half, heated

1½ teaspoons granulated chicken bouillon

¼ teaspoon dried thyme

½ teaspoon white pepper

⅓ cup dry sherry

1 pound crabmeat, lump preferred, picked over for shells and cartilage

THE TRAWL DOOR'S SPICY RED CRAB SOUP

2 tablespoons peanut oil

1 cup chopped yellow onion

½ cup diced celery

½ cup diced carrots

½ cup seeded and diced green bell pepper

½ to 1 teaspoon red pepper flakes, to your taste

2 bay leaves

1 tablespoon finely chopped garlic

½ teaspoon Tabasco sauce

2 teaspoons Worcestershire sauce

Three 10.5-ounce cans reduced-sodium chicken broth

Two 32-ounce cans peeled whole tomatoes, undrained and roughly crushed

One 46-ounce can tomato juice

One 10-ounce box frozen corn, defrosted

¼ cup chopped fresh Italian parsley leaves

2 teaspoons Chesapeake Bay seasoning

2 pounds crabmeat, special, claw meat, or lump preferred, picked over for shells and cartilage

Oriental, North Carolina, is a sleepy boating town that has remained untouched by most of the hideous coastal development. Oriental is also one of the most important crabbing areas along the North Carolina coast. It used to be home to a wonderful seafood restaurant called the Trawl Door, which made a great tomato-based crab soup. This is as close as I could get to re-creating it. Alas, the restaurant is gone, a victim of its beautiful location on the water. Making this soup reminds me of my many visits there with my daughter and her Indian Princess tribe. Don't be put off by the number of ingredients; this is an easy dump-and-stir recipe.

SERVES 16 AS A FIRST COURSE OR 8 AS A MAIN COURSE

1. Heat a soup pot over medium-high heat and add the oil. When hot, add the onion, celery, carrots, and bell pepper and cook, stirring, until soft, about 8 minutes. Add the red pepper flakes, bay leaves, garlic, Tabasco, and Worcestershire and cook for 2 minutes. Add the broth, tomatoes, and tomato juice and bring to a boil. Reduce the heat to medium-low and simmer for about 1 hour.

2. Stir in the corn, parsley, and Bay seasoning and simmer for no more than 5 minutes.

3. Place 2 tablespoons of the crabmeat in each serving bowl and ladle the soup over the crabmeat. This keeps the crabmeat from overcooking and losing its flavor in the spiciness of the soup. Serve immediately.

Note: Any leftover soup can be frozen. Just defrost and reheat, then add the crabmeat to each serving.

Cold beet soup may get an "ugh" from you or your family, but I urge you to try this recipe in the hottest months of the summer. This recipe is based on one passed on to me by Delores Custer, my mentor as a food stylist and my travel guide, with her late husband, Art, through the cuisines of Manhattan. **SERVES 4 TO 6**

1. Put the beets in a large saucepan and add water to cover. Sprinkle with a little salt and bring to a boil. Reduce the heat to medium-low, cover, and let simmer until fork tender, 25 to 45 minutes. Drain, peel when cool enough to handle, and slice into rounds.

2. Melt the butter in a large saucepan or Dutch oven over medium heat. When it stops foaming, add the leek, carrot, celery, and onion and cook, stirring, until almost tender. Stir in the cooked beets, parsley, and beef broth. Cover, bring to a boil, reduce the heat to medium-low, and simmer for 10 minutes. Remove from the heat and let cool slightly.

3. Pour about 1 cup of the soup at a time into a blender or food processor and process until smooth. Pour the pureed soup into a large mixing bowl. Stir in the salt, pepper, and 4 tablespoons of the lemon juice. Cover with plastic wrap and refrigerate for at least 4 hours.

4. Gently mix the crabmeat, the remaining 2 tablespoons lemon juice, and a fair amount of black pepper together, taking care to keep the crabmeat in lumps.

5. Pour the cold soup into chilled serving bowls. Divide the crabmeat mixture evenly among the bowls and garnish with a dollop of the sour cream and a sprinkling of chives, if using.

6 medium-size beets, scrubbed and trimmed, leaving 1 inch of the stem and root intact

¼ cup (½ stick) unsalted butter

1 large leek (white and light green parts), washed well and sliced crosswise

1 medium-size carrot, sliced into rounds

2 stalks celery, sliced

1 medium-size yellow onion, chopped

2 tablespoons chopped fresh Italian parsley leaves

Three 10.5-ounce cans reduced-sodium beef broth

½ teaspoon kosher salt

⅛ teaspoon freshly ground black pepper

6 tablespoons fresh lemon juice

1 pound crabmeat (peekytoe is really great), picked over for shells and cartilage

1 cup sour cream

Chopped fresh chives for garnish (optional)

eula mae's seafood gumbo

5 tablespoons vegetable oil

1 pound medium-size fresh okra, bottoms trimmed and cut into ¼-inch-thick rounds, or one 16-ounce package frozen sliced okra, defrosted

4 teaspoons distilled white vinegar

1 cup all-purpose flour

1¼ cups chopped yellow onion

1¼ cups chopped scallions (white and green parts)

1 clove garlic, minced

2 cups seeded and chopped green bell pepper

1 cup chopped celery

2 tablespoons chopped fresh Italian parsley leaves

One 32-ounce can peeled whole tomatoes, undrained and chopped

1 cup chopped boiled ham

2 cups water (see Note)

2 bay leaves

2 sprigs fresh thyme

1 tablespoon Worcestershire sauce

1 teaspoon Tabasco sauce, plus more for serving

1 teaspoon kosher salt

1 pound medium-size shrimp, peeled and deveined

1 pound crabmeat, lump preferred, picked over for shells and cartilage

Cooked long-grain white rice

every cook in south Louisiana has a version of seafood gumbo—many have 2 or 3. But on Avery Island, Eula Mae Doré's slow-cooked seafood gumbo takes the prize. This recipe is from her book, *Eula Mae's Cajun Kitchen: Cooking Through the Seasons on Avery Island*, which is overflowing with good eatin' recipes. Gumbo, the famous roux-based stew of Louisiana, is made with anything from squirrel to duck, but it's the seafood form that's really special. Don't be wary of making a roux; it's very simple. **SERVES 6 TO 8**

1. Heat 3 tablespoons of the oil in a medium-size skillet (not cast-iron, which will discolor the okra) over medium heat. Add the okra and cook, stirring frequently, for about 30 minutes. Add the vinegar and cook until the okra is no longer ropy or slimy and is lightly browned, about 10 minutes. Remove from the heat and set aside.

2. Heat the remaining 2 tablespoons oil in a large, heavy pot or Dutch oven over medium heat for 2 minutes. Add the flour and cook, stirring slowly and constantly, to make a dark brown roux (almost the color of chocolate). Add the onion, 1 cup of the scallions, the garlic, bell peppers, celery, and 1 tablespoon of the parsley. Cook, stirring often, until the vegetables are tender and light golden brown, about 10 minutes. Add the tomatoes, ham, okra, water, bay leaves, thyme, Worcestershire, Tabasco, and salt. Reduce the heat to medium-low, cover, and simmer for 45 minutes.

3. Add the shrimp and crabmeat and simmer until the shrimp turn pink, 8 to 10 minutes. Remove and discard the bay leaf and thyme. Garnish with the remaining ¼ cup scallions and 1 tablespoon parsley.

4. Serve over rice and pass additional Tabasco at the table.

Note: If you can get shrimp with the heads on, try making shrimp stock and replace the water in this recipe with stock for extra flavor. Put the shrimp heads and peelings in a large pot with the peel from the onion and a rib or two of celery. Add water to cover and bring to a boil. Reduce the heat to medium-low and simmer for 1 hour. Strain the stock and use immediately, or store in an airtight container in the freezer for up to 3 months.

creative crab salads

In the South, with its bounty of blue crabs during the summer, crab salad regularly shows up at bridge clubs, church circle meetings, poolside parties—well, you get the point. They have long been a focal point of Southern entertaining, with the hostess often splurging for the fine lump crabmeat befitting the star of the show.

On the West Coast, during the fall and winter, Dungeness crab is at its peak. Cold crab dressed with a simple mayonnaise and served on lettuce is traditional in many San Francisco homes on Christmas Eve and as part of a Christmas Day lunch.

The recipes in this chapter run the gamut of first-course to full-meal salads. I think you'll be surprised by the number of refreshing ways crab can please your palate.

Throughout much of this book, I stay away from specifying the exact type or grade of crabmeat to use, letting you choose what is freshest and most commonly available in your area. That holds true for this chapter as well, but with salads, the higher the quality of the crabmeat and the larger the lump, the more satisfied you will be with the results. Fresh Dungeness, lump blue, and especially peekytoe crab are well suited for salad preparations. Stay away from the canned and frozen stuff for these recipes.

Ben Barker's marinated Lump crab salad

Marinated crab:

1 pound lump (not Venezuelan, not backfin) blue crabmeat, picked over for shells and cartilage

½ cup finely diced shallots

1 jalapeño, seeded and finely diced

Grated zest of 2 lemons

¼ cup fresh lemon juice

2 tablespoons slivered fresh tarragon leaves

¼ cup slivered fresh Italian parsley leaves

½ cup fruity extra virgin olive oil

Kosher salt and freshly ground black pepper to taste

Tabasco sauce to taste

Louis dressing:

2 very fresh large egg yolks, at room temperature (see Note)

2 tablespoons tarragon vinegar

2 tablespoons fresh lemon juice

1 tablespoon Dijon mustard

1 cup olive oil (a blend is okay)

2 tablespoons sambal oelek or Asian chili paste (available in the Asian foods section of most large supermarkets)

1 tablespoon ketchup

1 tablespoon sour cream

Kosher salt to taste

Ben Barker is chef and co-owner with his wife, Karen, of the Magnolia Grill restaurant in Durham, North Carolina. Now maybe Durham, which is one corner of Research Triangle Park, doesn't pop right up on your food map, but the Magnolia Grill can hold its own and even outshine some of the top dining stops in the country. Ben and Karen are each James Beard Award winners, and they have received numerous other awards as well. I've accused Ben of dreaming in flavor, and his take on crab Louis certainly highlights his intense love of only the best ingredients. Don't let the length of this recipe hold you back; the reward is outstanding. **SERVES 10**

1. To make the marinated crab, combine all the ingredients in a large mixing bowl and toss gently to mix. Adjust the flavor with additional lemon juice and/or olive oil as necessary; it should be bright, tangy, and olivaceous. You can prepare this part of the recipe up to 1 day in advance. Cover with plastic wrap and keep refrigerated until needed. Bring to room temperature for 30 minutes before proceeding. Gently toss to blend the ingredients.

2. To make the dressing, whisk together the egg yolks, vinegar, lemon juice, and mustard in a medium-size mixing bowl. Add the oil in a steady stream, whisking until the dressing thickens. Fold in the sambal oelek, ketchup, and sour cream. Season with salt, then refrigerate until ready to use.

3. Keep each component of the chopped salad separate. All the ingredients except the avocado may be prepared up to 1 day in advance and refrigerated until assembly. Cut the avocado right before you need it.

4. To serve the salad, arrange 3 lettuce leaves on each serving plate in a spoke pattern. Place an avocado slice between the leaves. Place a 2-inch steel or PVC ring mold in the center of the spoke pattern.

5. Combine all the chopped salad ingredients in a medium-size mixing bowl. Add half the dressing, season with salt, and toss gently to coat thoroughly. Check the seasoning, then firmly pack some of the salad into each ring mold to a depth of 1¼ inches. (It is important to pack firmly for stability.) Add ⅓ cup of the marinated crab and pack it down firmly. Holding the salad in place, lift the ring mold.

6. Lightly season the avocado and lettuce with salt and pepper. Drizzle the remaining dressing over the lettuce, avocado, and crab salad. Garnish each salad with 2 or 3 chervil sprigs, then drip a little tarragon oil around the perimeter, if you are so inclined. Serve immediately.

Note: Because the dressing contains raw eggs, make sure to use the freshest eggs possible, purchased from a reliable grocer, to minimize any chance of salmonella.

---

roasting peppers

to roast a pepper, char it on all sides over a gas flame, holding it with metal tongs. Or preheat the oven to 400°F and roast the pepper, turning it occasionally, until all sides are charred. With either method, place the hot pepper in a zippered-top plastic bag and let it steam for 15 to 20 minutes. The charred skin will scrape off easily.

Chopped vegetable salad:

1 cup finely diced fennel bulb, blanched in boiling water until crisp-tender and drained

1 medium-size red bell pepper, roasted (see box), peeled, seeded, and finely diced

1 medium-size yellow bell pepper, roasted, peeled, seeded, and finely diced

1 cup peeled, seeded, and finely diced ripe tomatoes (Roma or plum tomatoes are best)

1 cup haricots verts or very thin green beans, ends trimmed, blanched in boiling water until crisp-tender, drained, and sliced crosswise ⅛ inch thick

½ cup frisée, inner white and yellow leaves only, sliced crosswise ¼ inch thick

1 firm but ripe Hass avocado, peeled, pitted, finely diced, and tossed with a little fresh lemon juice

Kosher salt to taste

Baby red oak leaf lettuce (3 leaves per plate)

Ripe but firm Hass avocado slices (3 per plate), about ⅛ inch thick

Kosher salt and freshly ground black pepper to taste

Fresh chervil sprigs for garnish

Tarragon oil (optional) for garnish

GULF COAST CRAB-RICE SALAD

3 cups cooked white rice

One 10-ounce box frozen tiny green peas, defrosted

¾ cup crème fraîche

2 tablespoons extra virgin olive oil

2 teaspoons fresh lemon juice

1 teaspoon Cajun seasoning

1 teaspoon sugar

½ teaspoon onion powder

½ to 1 teaspoon hot pepper sauce, to your taste

Kosher salt and freshly ground black pepper to taste

1 pound crabmeat, special or better preferred, picked over for shells and cartilage

Lettuce leaves

Folks along the Gulf coast consume copious amounts of rice with their gumbos and other Creole favorites—really, with anything they can think of. There's always leftover rice, but cooks in the Deep South use everything; nothing goes to waste. Crab and rice commingle perfectly, mainly because of their slightly different textures, and make a cool and refreshing salad for a hot summer day. This is a straightforward recipe—a marriage of many I've had. I've goosed it up a bit with crème fraîche, but you can substitute plain yogurt or sour cream (thinned with a little milk) if that's easier. If you want more heat, you can use up to 1 teaspoon hot pepper sauce without overpowering the crab. **SERVES 6 TO 8**

Stir together the rice, peas, crème fraîche, oil, lemon juice, Cajun seasoning, sugar, onion powder, and hot pepper sauce. Season with salt and pepper, then gently fold in the crabmeat. Serve on lettuce leaves.

crab salad with asparagus and lime vinaigrette

asparagus is the first gift of spring, with an abundance of fresh crab coming closely on its heels. Although lemon is the standard seasoning for asparagus, lime makes an exemplary statement in this light but refreshing vinaigrette. The avocado is a nice textural foil but can be omitted. Using peekytoe or Dungeness crab adds visual interest to the salad, but lump or jumbo lump blue crab also is excellent. **MAKES 4 SERVINGS**

1. To make the vinaigrette, whisk together the lime juice, vinegar, lime zest, ginger, and honey in a small mixing bowl. Whisk in the oil until it thickens. Season with salt and pepper and set aside.

2. To make the salad, bring a pot of water to a boil and cook the asparagus until just tender, about 5 minutes. Immediately scoop them out of the boiling water and plunge into a bowl of ice water to stop the cooking and set their color. When the asparagus are cold, drain, then toss with 3 tablespoons of the vinaigrette. Set aside.

3. In a medium-size mixing bowl, toss the crabmeat with 3 tablespoons of the vinaigrette and set aside. In a large bowl, toss the lettuce leaves with 3 tablespoons of the vinaigrette.

4. To serve, divide the dressed lettuce among 4 large chilled plates. Place an avocado half on top of the lettuce on each plate and drizzle the avocado with a little vinaigrette. Divide the dressed asparagus among the plates, setting them next to each avocado half. Divide the dressed crabmeat among the plates, placing it on the asparagus. Serve immediately.

Note: The vinaigrette may be made 1 day ahead and the asparagus may be cooked (but not dressed) a few hours ahead. Keep both in the refrigerator.

Lime vinaigrette:

3 tablespoons fresh lime juice

1 tablespoon unseasoned rice vinegar

2 teaspoons grated lime zest

1½ teaspoons peeled and finely minced fresh ginger

1½ teaspoons honey

½ cup olive oil (not extra virgin)

Kosher salt and freshly ground black pepper to taste

Salad:

1 pound asparagus, bottoms snapped off

1 pound crabmeat, picked over for shells and cartilage

2 heads Bibb lettuce (about ½ pound each), leaves separated, washed, and dried

2 ripe but firm Hass avocados, halved lengthwise, pitted, and peeled

Greek salad dressing:

¾ cup olive oil

¼ cup red wine vinegar

1 teaspoon kosher salt

1 teaspoon dried oregano

Freshly ground black pepper
  to taste

Salad:

1 head romaine lettuce, sliced
  crosswise into thin ribbons

1 European cucumber, thinly
  sliced

1 small red onion, halved and
  thinly sliced into half moons

3 ripe plum tomatoes, cut into
  wedges and seeded

1 cup Greek black olives, drained
  and pitted

4 ounces feta cheese, crumbled

1 pound crabmeat, lump
  preferred, picked over for
  shells and cartilage

much to my surprise, Greek salads with crabmeat are widespread throughout the Chesapeake Bay region, and it is easy to see why: the essence of Greek cuisine intertwines with the cool richness of the crab. For a light supper after a summer day of outdoor activities, it's hard to do better than this. Serve it with toasted pita bread. **SERVES 6**

1. To make the dressing, whisk together all the ingredients in a small mixing bowl until thick.

2. To make the salad, combine the lettuce, cucumber, onion, and tomatoes in a large mixing bowl. Whisk the dressing and drizzle ¼ cup over the salad. Toss well. If necessary, add ¼ cup more and toss until all the greens are nicely coated.

3. Divide the salad among 6 chilled salad plates. Divide the olives, feta, and crabmeat among the plates, arranging them on top of the salad. Whisk the remaining dressing and drizzle 2 tablespoons on each salad.

GALATOIRE'S-STYLE CHOPPED CRAB SALAD

Galatoire's is one of the oldest, best, and most famous restaurants in New Orleans. Little has changed in this family-owned establishment since Jean Galatoire set up shop in 1905. The menu is French Creole, with a heavy accent on seafood. No food lover's trip to the Big Easy would be complete without a stop here.

This is my take on the restaurant's chopped salad, a combination of crab and shrimp. And even if you think you don't like anchovies, try them here. The extra zing they provide makes for a tasty dance with the sweetness of the crabmeat. **SERVES 6**

1. To make the dressing, whisk together all the ingredients in a small mixing bowl and set aside.

2. To make the salad, divide the lettuce, tomatoes, crab, and shrimp evenly among 6 chilled salad plates. Pour a little dressing on top.

3. Peel and quarter the eggs. Place 2 quarters on each salad. Crisscross 2 anchovy fillets over each salad. Serve immediately, passing the remaining dressing at the table.

Creole mustard dressing:

⅔ cup vegetable oil

⅓ cup red wine vinegar

½ cup Creole or other grainy mustard

Salad:

1 head iceberg lettuce, heavy stems removed and remaining lettuce chopped

2 ripe plum tomatoes, seeded and chopped

1 pound crabmeat, backfin blue preferred, picked over for shells and cartilage

1 pound large shrimp, peeled, deveined, cooked in boiling water just until pink, and drained

3 hard-boiled large eggs, cooled

12 anchovy fillets, drained

Dungeness crab salad with winter citrus and avocado

2 cups fresh orange juice

Kosher salt and freshly ground black pepper to taste

1 cup extra virgin olive oil, plus more for drizzling

3 blood oranges, peeled and cut into individual sections

2 limes, peeled and cut into individual sections

2 tangerines, peeled and cut into individual sections

1 grapefruit, peeled and cut into individual sections

1 lemon, peeled and cut into individual sections

2 precooked Dungeness crabs (2 to 2½ pounds each), picked of their meat (see page 19)

2 tablespoons minced fresh chives

1 ripe but firm Hass avocado, halved lengthwise, pitted, peeled, and sliced into half moons

3 cups mixed salad greens

Winter brings not only the richest-tasting Dungeness crab of the year, but also an abundance of citrus fruits at the peak of their flavor. This salad is lightly dressed with orange-infused olive oil, marrying the citrus sections, greens, and crab beautifully. Use whatever citrus fruits you like or are most available in your area. But if you can locate blood oranges, you'll be in for a treat for your palate and your eyes. **SERVES 4**

1. Pour the orange juice into a small nonreactive saucepan and simmer over medium heat until reduced to a thick syrup, 5 to 10 minutes. Strain through a fine-mesh strainer into a small mixing bowl, season with salt and pepper, and gradually whisk in the oil. Set aside.

2. Combine the blood orange, lime, tangerine, grapefruit, and lemon segments in a medium-size mixing bowl and set aside. Put the crabmeat in another medium-size mixing bowl, add ½ cup of the orange-flavored oil, sprinkle with the chives, and toss gently but thoroughly. Taste and correct the seasonings.

3. Divide the avocado slices among 4 serving plates and spoon some of the citrus salad on top. Spoon the crab on top of the citrus. Scatter the greens on top of each serving, drizzle with a little olive oil, and finish by drizzling with some of the remaining orange-flavored oil. Serve immediately.

inspired crab cobb salad with apple wood–smoked bacon

Anchovy-garlic dressing:

One 2-ounce can anchovy fillets, drained and chopped

1 tablespoon chopped garlic

1 very fresh medium-size egg (see Note on page 83)

¼ cup chopped yellow onion

½ cup freshly grated Parmesan cheese

1 teaspoon freshly ground black pepper

2 tablespoons red wine vinegar

½ cup plus 2 tablespoons olive oil

Kosher salt to taste (optional)

Salad:

6 cups torn romaine lettuce

1½ pounds crabmeat, jumbo lump backfin preferred, picked over for shells and cartilage

6 hard-boiled large eggs, peeled and roughly chopped

12 strips apple wood– or double-smoked bacon, cooked until crisp, drained on paper towels, and crumbled

3 ripe but firm Hass avocados, halved lengthwise, pitted, peeled, sliced into half moons, and brushed with a little fresh lemon juice

3 cups cubed Gruyère or mild blue cheese

Indeed I was inspired when my editor, Pam Hoenig, started describing a crab cobb salad she had enjoyed at Ella Brennan's famous Commander's Palace in New Orleans. It was a lunch lodged vividly in her memory, and she gushed with details, making me instantly hungry. When people talk with me in great detail and excitement about a food or dish they have had, I want to know more. After a few conversations with the folks at this highly regarded eatery (Brennan recognized Emeril's talent long before the rest of us did), I had a pretty good idea of what to do. Brennan's version changes often, so design this salad your way. Just be sure to use a good lump crabmeat. Although it's not too different from the Brown Derby restaurant's original cobb salad, the anchovy-based dressing really makes this salad sing.

SERVES 6

1. To make the dressing, place the anchovies, garlic, egg, onion, Parmesan, pepper, and vinegar in a blender or food processor and pulse to combine. With the machine running, slowly add the oil through the feed tube, processing until the dressing thickens. Taste and add salt, if desired. This can be made up to 3 days ahead and refrigerated.

2. To make the salad, place 1 cup of the lettuce on each of 6 chilled dinner plates. In a row across the lettuce, place ¼ pound of the crabmeat. Divide the eggs evenly among the plates, arranging them along the crabmeat on each plate. Do the same with the bacon, avocado, and Gruyère, arranging them in rows one after the other. Pass the dressing and let the diners toss and dress their own salads to their liking.

swan oyster Depot's crab Louis

I never make a trip to San Francisco without a stop at Swan Oyster Depot. This throwback to another era, located in the Russian Hill section of the city, was founded in 1912 and bought in 1946 by Sal Sancimino, whose family still runs the place today. The 20-plus stools (no tables) are almost always taken, so be patient. Your reward will be the finest oyster cocktail on either coast, as well as the freshest Dungeness crab dishes around.

Crab Louis is a West Coast iconic dish, but its roots are cloudy. Some say it originated at the Olympic Club in Seattle; others point to the St. Francis Hotel in San Francisco. Crab Louis consists of chopped lettuce with a pile of Dungeness crabmeat on top, dressed with a mayonnaise and chili sauce concoction. Like crab cake recipes on the Chesapeake Bay, there are many variations on this theme. Mike Sancimino walked me through his restaurant's crab Louis, and I urge you to try it, though it won't be the same as eating it at the counter amid Swan's whirlwind of activity and banter.

SERVES 4

2 precooked Dungeness crabs (2 to 2½ pounds each)

1½ cups mayonnaise

½ cup ketchup

2 tablespoons pitted and minced black olives

2 tablespoons sweet pickle relish

2 tablespoons minced white onion

1 hard-boiled large egg, peeled and minced

Kosher salt and freshly ground pepper to taste

1 head iceberg lettuce, heavy stems removed and remaining lettuce chopped

1 lemon, quartered, for garnish

1. Clean the crabs, then pick the meat from the shells (see page 19), keeping the leg meat separate from the body meat. Refrigerate until ready to use.

2. In a medium-size mixing bowl, mix together the mayonnaise, ketchup, olives, relish, onion, and egg, then season with salt and pepper.

3. Divide the lettuce among 4 serving plates. Sprinkle the crab body meat over the lettuce. Spoon some of the dressing over the crab and place 2 leg sections on top of each serving. Garnish each with a lemon wedge and serve immediately.

tuscan crab panzanella

4 to 6 slices day-old French or similar bread, cubed

6 ripe plum tomatoes, seeded and cut into eighths

2 large cloves garlic, thinly sliced

1 small cucumber, seeded and thinly sliced

1 medium-size red onion, chopped (about 1 cup)

2 tablespoons chopped fresh Italian parsley leaves

½ cup extra virgin olive oil

2 tablespoons distilled white vinegar

1 teaspoon balsamic vinegar

1 cup loosely packed fresh basil leaves

¼ cup capers, drained

1 pound crabmeat, picked over for shells and cartilage

Kosher salt and freshly ground black pepper to taste

Panzanella is simply a bread salad—another way the ingenious Italians have of using everything, including day-old bread. I fell in love with this concept while taking an Italian cooking class at the Culinary Institute of America in Hyde Park, New York. Vibrant and loud, with great texture and color, this recipe includes the usual ingredients of this Tuscan favorite and adds the twist of crabmeat. Lump or claw, Dungeness, blue, or Jonah—all are good choices. **SERVES 4**

1. Toast the bread cubes in a dry, medium-size nonstick skillet over medium heat until lightly browned on all sides. Transfer to a large salad bowl.

2. Add the tomatoes, garlic, cucumber, onion, parsley, oil, and vinegars to the bread. Toss and let sit for about 1 hour at room temperature.

3. When ready to serve, tear the basil into bite-size pieces and add to the bowl. Mix in the capers. Divide the salad among 4 bowls and top each with about one-quarter of the crabmeat. Season with salt and pepper and serve immediately.

THE CRAB CLAW'S DIETER'S DELIGHT

To call this a diet plate is almost false advertising. The idea came from the menu of one of Maryland's most famous crab houses—the Crab Claw in the charming town of St. Michaels. After a week of eating my way through the Eastern Shore, I decided to stop, for the second time, at this well-run restaurant. The Dieter's Delight Plate seemed a good choice for my expanding waistline, so I ordered one. What arrived at my table was a mound of jumbo lump crabmeat surrounded by fruit and some raspberry yogurt for dipping. It truly was inspired simplicity. Who knew that bananas and crab tasted so good together? When you want to beat the heat and add some fruit to your diet, fix this salad. **SERVES 4**

Divide the lettuce among 4 dinner plates. Put ½ cup of the crabmeat in the center of each plate. Surround the crabmeat with ½ cup of each fruit. Divide the yogurt among 4 ramekins and serve on the side.

½ head iceberg lettuce, heavy stems removed and remaining lettuce torn

2 cups crabmeat, jumbo lump backfin preferred, picked over for shells and cartilage

2 cups cantaloupe chunks

2 cups honeydew melon chunks

2 cups fresh pineapple chunks

2 cups sliced bananas

2 cups hulled and sliced fresh strawberries

1 cup raspberry or strawberry yogurt

THe eLUSIVe PerFeCT CraB Cake

Is there such a thing as the perfect crab cake? You bet there is, and every fifth person you meet has a different opinion of what exactly that is. Trying to decide who has the best crab cake is akin to discussing whether there were aliens at Roswell. People will never agree. Somewhere in this chapter, though, I hope you find your elusive perfect crab cake. But I'm willing to bet that the recipes you try along the way won't be too shabby either.

These recipes were inspired by folks and restaurants throughout the crabbing regions of the United States. You may be surprised by the lack of seasonings. When crab is fresh and in season, little is needed to enhance its naturally sweet flavor. But if you want a little more pop, don't hesitate to ratchet each recipe up to your own flavor quotient.

Here are a couple of hints before you start. First, follow the refrigeration instructions in the recipes. This time in the fridge allows the flavors to meld and helps the cakes hold together, making them easier to handle. It also plays a role in the cooking process, allowing the outside of the cakes to get crispy but keeping the inside moist and creamy.

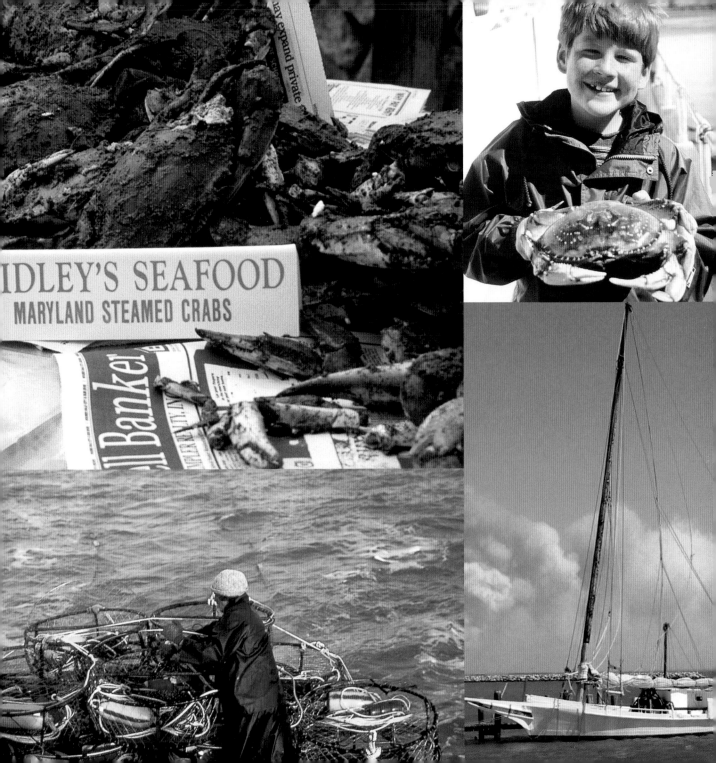

Second, try using an ice cream scoop to form your cakes. I use a #78, like the ones they use in school cafeterias, to keep my cakes at about ⅓ cup. I'd rather serve each diner 2 smaller cakes than 1 large one, so for me 1 pound of crabmeat averages 8 cakes, feeding 4 to 6 people.

Third, handle the cakes gently, taking care not to pack them too much, as this will make them tough and affect their texture. Finally, you can keep cooked crab cakes in a low oven (250° to 300°F) for about 20 minutes, but any longer than that will dry them out—a true crime against humanity and a damn waste of perfectly good crabmeat.

Just because a recipe calls for one type of crabmeat doesn't mean you can't use another. Most of these recipes will work fine with just about any type or grade of crabmeat. I love to mix lump blue crab with claw meat, which yields great texture and taste.

Crab cakes can be fried, sautéed, or broiled. In the recipes that say to broil, use only that method. In all the other recipes, the cooking method is up to you, even if another method is suggested.

So go buy some crabmeat and have fun.

eastern bay crab cakes

Pulling a crab cake recipe out of the watermen or their families in the Crisfield, Maryland, area was tough. Most would say that crab cakes are "too much trouble" and offer another crab recipe. When pushed, a simplicity began to emerge. Along this part of the Chesapeake Bay, the flavor of the crabmeat is paramount, and little is done to change it. "Take an egg, some melted butter, lemon juice, and parsley, then just mix it with some bread crumbs or saltines" was a recipe I heard dozens of times. Simple. Nothing written down. After talking with the guys at Layton's Seafood, a fresh seafood retailer in Crisfield, Maryland, I came up with this recipe. Handle the cakes gently and be sure to refrigerate them as directed.

MAKES ABOUT 10 CRAB CAKES

1 large egg, lightly beaten

½ cup (1 stick) unsalted butter, melted

1 tablespoon fresh lemon juice

2 teaspoons Worcestershire sauce

1 cup roughly crushed saltines

1 pound crabmeat, backfin preferred, picked over for shells and cartilage

Canola oil for frying

Lemon wedges

Sauce of your choice

1. Mix the egg, melted butter, lemon juice, and Worcestershire together in a medium-size mixing bowl. Fold in the saltines until moist. *Fold* in the crabmeat *gently*. Form the mixture into 10 crab cakes, about ⅓ cup each, and place on a baking sheet covered with waxed paper. Cover and refrigerate for at least 1 hour (2 hours is better, and overnight is fine).

2. Heat about 1 inch of oil in a large, high-sided frying pan over medium heat until the oil shimmers but hasn't started to smoke, about 350°F. Fry the crab cakes in batches, taking care not to crowd them, until golden brown, about 4 minutes per side. Drain on paper towels or brown paper bags. (Draining on bags will give you a crisper crust.) Serve with lemon wedges and your favorite sauce.

Fred's Pretty Darn Close to Perfect Crab Cakes

2 large eggs

¼ cup buttermilk

¼ cup finely diced red onion

2 scallions (white and green parts), thinly sliced

2 tablespoons chopped fresh Italian parsley leaves

1 tablespoon seeded and finely diced red bell pepper

1 teaspoon Chesapeake Bay seasoning

½ teaspoon dry mustard

10 to 15 saltines, roughly crushed

1 pound crabmeat, lump or jumbo lump backfin preferred, picked over for shells and cartilage

2 tablespoons peanut or other neutral-tasting oil (not olive oil)

2 tablespoons unsalted butter

Gravy flour (such as Wondra) or all-purpose flour as needed

Tartar sauce, homemade (see page 101) or store-bought

I know, this is pretty brazen of me, but the one recipe I'm begged for most is my crab cakes. Up until now, I have casually dodged these requests. So for all the people who have asked, here it is—maybe. Please take the time to refrigerate the crab cakes at each point called for in the recipe. It will make your life much easier, and the crab cakes will look and taste better.

MAKES ABOUT 8 CRAB CAKES

1. Lightly beat the eggs and buttermilk together in small bowl and set aside.

2. In a large mixing bowl, combine the onion, scallions, parsley, bell pepper, Bay seasoning, and mustard. Mix in the saltines. Add the egg mixture and stir to combine. *Fold* in the crabmeat *gently*, trying to not break up the lumps. Cover and refrigerate for 2 hours.

3. Mold the crab mixture into 8 cakes and place on a baking sheet covered with waxed paper. Cover and refrigerate for at least 30 minutes or up to 4 hours.

4. Preheat the oven to 350°F.

5. Heat the oil and butter together in a large sauté pan or cast-iron skillet over medium-high heat. Once the butter has melted, sprinkle the tops of the crab cakes lightly with flour and place the cakes flour side down in the pan. Sprinkle the other side with flour. Cook until browned on the bottom, about 4 minutes. Carefully turn the crab cakes over. Place the pan in the oven and bake until heated through, 10 to 15 minutes.

6. Serve immediately, or turn off the oven and let sit in the oven for up to 30 minutes. Serve with tartar sauce on the side.

Faidley's World Famous Crab Cakes

½ cup mayonnaise

1 large egg, lightly beaten

1½ teaspoons Dijon mustard

1½ teaspoons prepared brown mustard

1 tablespoon Worcestershire sauce

½ teaspoon hot pepper sauce

1 cup roughly crushed saltines

1 pound crabmeat, lump preferred, picked over for shells and cartilage

Vegetable oil for frying

Tartar sauce (optional), homemade (recipe follows) or store-bought

There are lots of reasons to visit Baltimore, aka Charm City, but if you are a true crab freak, there is only one stop that is absolutely mandatory. In Lexington Market, you'll find Faidley Seafood. Faidley's has won more "best crab cake" awards than anyplace else on earth, and with good reason. The restaurant serves 3 types of crab cakes: one made with all claw meat, one with backfin, and, my favorite, a jumbo lump crab cake that could double for a baseball from the Orioles' Camden Yards. Faidley's is family run, with Nancy Faidley Devine the keeper of the cake recipe. At 67, she makes every one of the crab cakes they sell. Mrs. Devine says that making crab cakes is much like making a good pie dough—handle it too much and you'll ruin the texture. She also uses no imported crabmeat, which she considers "tasteless." As for this recipe, Mrs. Devine is secretive about the exact measurements. Her husband, Bill, told *New York Times* reporter R. W. Apple, Jr., "I sleep with her, and she won't tell me." One feature that I believe makes her crab cakes so good is the frugal use of Chesapeake Bay seasoning. Mrs. Devine, I hope you approve. **MAKES 8 CRAB CAKES**

1. Stir together the mayonnaise, egg, mustards, Worcestershire, and hot pepper sauce in a medium-size mixing bowl. Fold in the saltines until moist. *Fold* in the crabmeat *gently*. Cover and refrigerate for 30 minutes.

2. Shape the mixture into 8 patties, about ⅓ cup each. Place on a baking sheet lined with waxed paper, cover, and refrigerate for at least 1 hour or up to 4 hours.

3. Heat about 1½ inches of oil in a large, high-sided skillet over medium-high heat until the oil shimmers but hasn't started to smoke, about 350°F.

Fry the crab cakes in batches, taking care not to crowd them, until golden brown, about 4 minutes per side. Drain on paper towels or brown paper bags. (Draining on bags will give you a crisper crust.) Serve with tartar sauce, if desired.

Variations: This recipe takes kindly to other cooking methods. To sauté the crab cakes, cook in 3 tablespoons unsalted butter or vegetable oil in a large nonstick skillet over medium-high heat until golden brown, about 4 minutes per side. To broil the crab cakes, preheat the broiler, place the cakes on a large baking sheet, and broil until golden brown, 4 to 5 minutes per side.

tartar sauce

Depending on the type of pickles you use, you can create a regional specialty. Add dill pickles, and you have more of a Northern-style sauce—the type that many companies mimic on grocery store shelves. Making it with sweet pickles brings this sauce to the South, where sweetness reigns supreme. I like to use a little of both, just to mix things up.

MAKES ABOUT 1½ CUPS

1 cup mayonnaise

½ cup finely chopped dill pickles or sweet pickles

¼ cup minced yellow onion

2 tablespoons chopped fresh Italian parsley leaves

1 tablespoon dill pickle or sweet pickle juice

Mix everything together in a medium-size mixing bowl. Cover and refrigerate for at least 1 hour before serving. This sauce will keep in the refrigerator for 3 to 4 days.

acadian crab and crawfish cakes

Crab and crawfish cakes:

1 tablespoon olive oil

⅓ cup seeded and diced red bell pepper

⅓ cup diced celery

⅓ cup finely chopped yellow onion

¼ teaspoon kosher salt

10 grinds of black pepper

1½ tablespoons Cajun seasoning

1 tablespoon finely chopped garlic

2 large eggs, lightly beaten

2 tablespoons Creole or other grainy mustard

½ cup dry bread crumbs

¼ pound frozen precooked crawfish tails, defrosted and drained well (see headnote)

1 pound crabmeat, lump preferred, picked over for shells and cartilage

Breading:

1 cup dry bread crumbs

2 tablespoons Cajun seasoning

1 cup all-purpose flour

1 large egg, lightly beaten

¼ cup water

Canola or peanut oil for frying

Creole Tartar Sauce (optional; recipe follows)

Louisiana food writer Pableaux Johnson keeps me posted on all things Creole and Cajun. With his help, I have stuffed the best of south Louisiana foodways into these crab cakes. The "holy trinity" of bell pepper, celery, and onion is present, and just for good measure, so are crawfish tails. Frozen precooked crawfish tails are available almost everywhere now in the frozen fish section of large supermarkets. Most likely you'll find a ½-pound bag. Defrost the tails, drain well, and squeeze as much liquid out as you can. The resulting meat will be just right for this recipe. These crab cakes will light up your taste buds. **MAKES 8 TO 10 CRAB CAKES**

1. To make the cakes, heat the oil in a medium-size sauté pan or cast-iron skillet over medium-high heat. Add the bell pepper, celery, onion, salt, black pepper, and Cajun seasoning and cook for about 2 minutes, stirring well. Add the garlic and cook, stirring, until you can just smell the garlic.

2. Transfer to a medium-size mixing bowl. Rapidly stir in the eggs. Add the mustard and bread crumbs, stirring until the crumbs are moist. *Fold* in the crawfish tails and crabmeat *gently*. Refrigerate while you set up the breading process.

3. To bread the cakes, combine the bread crumbs and 1 tablespoon of the Cajun seasoning in a pie plate or shallow bowl. Combine the flour and remaining 1 tablespoon Cajun seasoning in another pie plate or bowl. Beat the egg and water together in a third pie plate or bowl.

4. Form the crab mixture into 8 to 10 cakes, about ⅓ cup each. Dredge the cakes with the seasoned flour, dip into the egg wash, and then coat

evenly with the bread crumbs, shaking off any excess. Place on a baking sheet lined with waxed paper, cover, and refrigerate for about 2 hours.

5. Preheat the oven to 300°F.

6. Heat about 1 inch of oil in a large, high-sided skillet over medium heat until the oil shimmers but hasn't started to smoke, about 350°F. Fry the crab cakes in batches, taking care not to crowd them, until golden brown, about 4 minutes per side. Drain on paper towels or brown paper bags. (Draining on bags will give you a crisper crust.) Transfer to an ovenproof plate and keep warm in the oven while you cook the remaining cakes. Serve warm with tartar sauce, if desired.

creole tartar sauce

What makes a tartar sauce Creole is the use of a Creole or other grainy mustard. I bet you will find lots of uses for this bright sauce.
MAKES ABOUT 1 CUP

Combine all the ingredients in a small bowl. Refrigerate for at least 2 hours or up to overnight to let the flavors develop.

½ cup mayonnaise

2 tablespoons Creole or other grainy mustard

2 tablespoons dill pickle relish

2 tablespoons chopped scallions (white and green parts)

1 tablespoon fresh lemon juice

1 tablespoon chopped fresh dill

Crab cakes:

1 cup fresh or defrosted frozen corn kernels

⅓ cup mayonnaise

2 tablespoons prepared yellow mustard

¼ cup chopped fresh Italian parsley leaves

¼ teaspoon Worcestershire sauce

2 large eggs, lightly beaten

20 butter crackers (such as Ritz), roughly crushed

1 pound crabmeat, lump preferred, picked over for shells and cartilage

Chipotle mayonnaise:

1 cup mayonnaise

2 tablespoons chopped scallions (white and green parts)

1 tablespoon chopped chipotle chiles in adobo sauce, plus some of the sauce to taste

2 teaspoons fresh lime juice

1 teaspoon Creole or other grainy mustard

1 tablespoon chopped fresh cilantro leaves

2 tablespoons canola oil

2 tablespoons unsalted butter

The sweetness of corn and the richness of crab against a smoky mayonnaise is a taste experience you just don't want to miss. Try these cakes with middle-of-the-summer corn, fresh off the cob, when crabmeat is at its peak. They make for an exciting summer party feast. **MAKES 10 TO 12 CAKES**

1. To make the crab cakes, mix together the corn, mayonnaise, mustard, parsley, and Worcester-shire in a medium-size mixing bowl. Blend in the eggs and stir in the crackers until moist. *Fold* in the crabmeat *gently*. Cover and refrigerate for 30 minutes.

2. Form the mixture into 10 to 12 cakes, about ⅓ cup each. Place on a baking sheet covered with waxed paper, cover, and refrigerate for at least 2 hours or up to overnight.

3. To make the chipotle mayonnaise, combine the mayonnaise, scallions, chiles and sauce, lime juice, and mustard in a small bowl. Stir in the cilantro. Refrigerate for several hours or up to 3 days to allow the flavors to meld.

4. Preheat the oven to 300°F.

5. Heat the oil and butter together in a medium-size sauté pan or cast-iron skillet over medium heat. When the butter stops foaming, add half the cakes and cook until golden brown, about 4 minutes per side. Drain on paper towels or brown paper bags. (Draining on bags will give you a crisper crust.) Transfer to an ovenproof plate and keep warm in the oven while you cook the remaining cakes. Serve warm, with the mayonnaise on the side.

coastal crab cakes

along the sounds and coastal regions of the East where blue crabs are plentiful, you'll find locals making crab cakes similar to these. The crabmeat is the star, so use the best quality you can afford. Dungeness and Maine crab carry these cakes just as well as blue crab. If you like a little onion, bell pepper, or Chesapeake Bay seasoning in your crab cakes, go ahead and add it. **MAKES 6 CAKES**

1. Combine the mayonnaise, parsley, horseradish, and mustard in a medium-size mixing bowl. Whisk in the eggs, then add the bread, stirring to moisten. *Fold* in the crabmeat *gently* and season with salt and pepper. Cover and refrigerate for 30 minutes.

2. Form the mixture into 6 cakes, about ⅓ cup each. Place on a baking sheet lined with waxed paper, cover, and refrigerate for at least 2 hours or up to 4 hours.

3. Heat the butter and oil together in a large sauté pan or cast-iron skillet over medium-high heat. When the butter stops foaming, add the crab cakes and cook until golden brown, 4 to 5 minutes per side. Drain on paper towels or brown paper bags. (Draining on bags will give you a crisper crust.) Serve warm with tartar sauce, if desired, but you probably won't need it.

1 tablespoon mayonnaise

1 tablespoon chopped fresh Italian parsley leaves

1½ teaspoons prepared horseradish, drained

1 teaspoon prepared yellow mustard

2 large eggs, lightly beaten

2 slices white bread, chopped with a knife

1 pound crabmeat (I like a mixture of lump and claw meat), picked over for shells and cartilage

Kosher salt and freshly ground black pepper to taste

1 tablespoon unsalted butter

1 tablespoon canola oil

Tartar sauce (optional), homemade (see page 101) or store-bought

mendo bistro's award-winning crab cakes with tarragon aioli

ort Bragg, Noyo Harbor, and Mendocino, California, are hotbeds of Dungeness crab cookery, and competition among the area's chefs to develop the most creative recipes is fierce. Each January, during the Mendocino Crab & Wine Days festival, they go head-to-head at the crab cake cook-off. For 2 years in a row, Nicholas Petti, chef and co-owner with his wife, Jaimi Parsons, of Mendo Bistro in Fort Bragg, has taken home first prize for his "less is more" crab cakes. The "less" refers to the filler, because Dungeness crab is the prime player here. These crab cakes are in my top 5 of all restaurant crab cakes. Mendo Bistro serves the cakes over a simple cabbage salad, using the acidic vinegar and crisp cabbage to play off the rich crab and luxurious aioli. **MAKES 4 HUGE CAKES**

1. To make the aioli, place the egg yolks, garlic, lemon juice, salt, and Tabasco in a food processor or blender and process until everything is homogenized. Add the water and process for 15 seconds. With the machine running, slowly drizzle in the oil until the mixture comes together and thickens. Transfer to a bowl and stir in the tarragon. Cover and refrigerate until ready to use, up to 2 days.

2. To make the crab cakes, combine the crabmeat, panko, scallions, and ½ cup of the aioli. If the mixture holds together, that's great. If not, add more aioli. Form the mixture into four 3-inch-diameter cakes. Sprinkle some panko on a plate and place one side of each crab cake in the crumbs.

3. In a sauté pan or cast-iron skillet large enough to hold the cakes comfortably, heat the oil over medium-high heat until just smoking. Add

Tarragon aioli:

2 very fresh large egg yolks (see Note page 108)

3 cloves garlic, peeled

Juice of 1 lemon

½ teaspoon kosher salt

⅛ teaspoon Tabasco sauce

¼ cup very hot water

2 cups extra virgin olive oil

¼ cup finely chopped fresh tarragon leaves

Crab cakes:

1½ pounds Dungeness crabmeat, picked over for shells and cartilage

¾ cup panko (Japanese bread crumbs), plus more for coating

2 scallions (white and green parts), finely chopped

½ to ¾ cup tarragon aioli, as needed

2 tablespoons canola oil

Mendo Bistro's Cabbage Salad (page 108)

the crab cakes, crumb side down, and cook until golden brown, about 4 minutes. Turn the cakes, reduce the heat slightly, and cook until golden brown and heated through. Drain on paper towels or brown paper bags. (Draining on bags will give you a crisper crust.) Serve with the remaining tarragon aioli and the cabbage salad on the side.

Note: Because the aioli contains raw eggs, make sure to use the freshest eggs possible, purchased from a reliable grocer, to minimize any chance of salmonella.

MENDO BISTRO'S CABBAGE SALAD

1 medium-size head cabbage, outer leaves removed and cored

Sea salt to taste

1 bunch fresh chives, finely chopped

⅓ cup champagne vinegar

This cabbage salad is great with any seafood dish. **SERVES 8**

1. Thinly slice the cabbage. In a medium-size mixing bowl, toss the cabbage with a liberal amount of sea salt and let sit for 30 minutes.

2. Drain the liquid from the cabbage, rinse, and drain again. Toss with the chives and vinegar. Serve immediately, or refrigerate for up to 1 day.

Charleston Herb-Filled Crab Cakes

In the early days of Charleston, South Carolina, spices were an important part of the trade in this Southern port. The lively use of spices and herbs is very much present today in the cooking of this beautiful city and the surrounding low country. I was inspired by those traditions to create a crab cake with a vibrant, fresh taste. **MAKES 8 TO 10 CRAB CAKES**

1. Mix the mayonnaise, sour cream, mustard, horseradish, herbs, and zests together in a medium-size mixing bowl. Season with salt and pepper. Add the eggs and bread crumbs and mix until the crumbs are moist. *Fold* in the crabmeat *gently*. Cover and refrigerate for 30 minutes.

2. Form the mixture into 8 to 10 cakes, about ⅓ cup each. Place on a baking sheet lined with waxed paper, cover, and refrigerate for at least 2 hours or up to overnight.

3. Preheat the oven to 300°F.

4. Heat the oil and butter together in a large sauté pan or cast-iron skillet over medium-high heat. When the butter stops foaming, add half the crab cakes and cook until golden brown, about 4 minutes per side. Drain on paper towels or brown paper bags. (Draining on bags will give you a crisper crust.) Transfer to an ovenproof plate and keep warm in the oven while you cook the remaining crab cakes. Serve with lemon wedges and tartar sauce, if desired.

½ cup mayonnaise

¼ cup sour cream

2 tablespoons Dijon mustard

2 tablespoons prepared horseradish, drained

1 tablespoon chopped fresh mint leaves

1 tablespoon chopped fresh tarragon leaves

1 tablespoon chopped fresh chives

1 tablespoon chopped fresh Italian parsley leaves

1½ teaspoons chopped fresh rosemary leaves

1 tablespoon grated lemon zest

1 tablespoon grated orange zest

Kosher salt and freshly ground black pepper to taste

2 large eggs, lightly beaten

1 cup dry bread crumbs

1 pound crabmeat, jumbo lump backfin preferred, picked over for shells and cartilage

2 tablespoons canola oil

2 tablespoons unsalted butter

Lemon wedges (optional)

Tartar sauce (optional), homemade (see page 101) or store-bought

crab and lobster cakes

1 cup mayonnaise

2 large eggs, lightly beaten

½ teaspoon Chesapeake Bay seasoning

½ teaspoon dry mustard

1 tablespoon fresh lemon juice

1 tablespoon fresh lime juice

10 saltines, roughly crushed

½ pound crabmeat, jumbo lump backfin preferred, picked over for shells and cartilage

½ pound chopped cooked lobster meat, knuckle and tail meat preferred, picked over for shells and cartilage

1½ cups corn flake crumbs

¼ cup canola oil

2 tablespoons unsalted butter

Feeling flush? Need to impress someone? Or maybe you just want 2 of the finest tastes from the sea in 1 place. Restaurants have used lobster and crab together in cakes for a while, but these cakes are easy to make at home. This is the time to go for jumbo lump backfin crabmeat. Handle it very gently so as not to break up the lumps. I coat these cakes with corn flake crumbs, which seem to make the crab and lobster even sweeter than they already are. A corn relish or corn salad is a great side for these cakes. Bob Kinkead of Kinkead's in Washington, D.C., and Louis Osteen of Louis's on Pawleys Island, South Carolina, inspired this recipe with their own wonderful examples served in their restaurants. **MAKES ABOUT 8 CAKES**

1. Blend the mayonnaise and eggs together in a medium-size mixing bowl. Stir in the Bay seasoning, mustard, and juices. Stir in the saltines until moist. *Fold* in the crabmeat and lobster *gently.* Cover and refrigerate for 30 minutes.

2. Form the mixture into 8 cakes, about ⅓ cup each. Coat the cakes evenly with the corn flake crumbs and place on a baking sheet lined with waxed paper. Cover and refrigerate for at least 1 hour or up to 4 hours.

3. Heat the oil and butter together in a large sauté pan or cast-iron skillet over medium-high heat. When the butter stops foaming, slide the cakes into the pan and cook until golden brown, 3 to 4 minutes per side. Drain on paper towels or brown paper bags. (Draining on bags will give you a crisper crust.) Serve warm.

THAI CRAB CAKES WITH CHILI-GARLIC SAUCE

Serve with sliced or shredded cucumbers marinated in seasoned rice vinegar for a complete Southeast Asia experience. Fish sauce is available in the Asian foods section of most large supermarkets, as are panko and chili-garlic sauce. Otherwise, look for them in an Asian grocery. **MAKES 8 TO 10 CRAB CAKES**

1. To make the crab cakes, combine the chiles, cilantro, scallions, fish sauce, garlic, and tamari in a medium-size mixing bowl. Stir in the eggs, then the bread crumbs, mixing until moist. *Fold* in the crabmeat *gently* (your hands will work best in this recipe).

2. Sprinkle the panko on a plate. Form the crab mixture into 8 to 10 cakes, about ⅓ cup each, and coat both sides with the panko. Place on a baking sheet lined with waxed paper, cover, and refrigerate for at least 30 minutes or up to 4 hours.

3. To make the sauce, combine the sugar, water, vinegar, garlic, and salt in a small saucepan and bring to a boil. Stir to dissolve the sugar and salt; reduce the heat to low. Simmer until reduced slightly, 15 to 20 minutes. Remove from the heat and stir in the chili-garlic sauce. Let cool to room temperature before serving.

4. Heat about 2 tablespoons of the oil in a large sauté pan or cast-iron skillet over medium-high heat. Cook the crab cakes a few at a time, taking care not to crowd them, until golden brown, 4 to 5 minutes per side. Drain on paper towels or brown paper bags. (Draining on bags will give you a crisper crust.) Serve warm with the sauce.

Crab cakes:

3 serrano or Thai chiles or 2 jalapeños, seeded and minced

2 tablespoons chopped fresh cilantro leaves

2 tablespoons chopped scallions (white and green parts)

1 tablespoon fish sauce

1 tablespoon minced garlic

2 teaspoons tamari or other low-sodium soy sauce

2 large eggs, lightly beaten

1 cup dry bread crumbs

1 pound Dungeness crabmeat, picked over for shells and cartilage

⅓ cup panko (Japanese bread crumbs)

Chili-garlic sauce:

1 cup sugar

½ cup water

½ cup distilled white vinegar

1 tablespoon finely minced garlic

1 teaspoon kosher salt

1 tablespoon chili-garlic sauce

2 to 3 tablespoons canola oil

veggie crab cakes

Crab cakes:

2 cups broccoli slaw mix
(in the produce section of
most large supermarkets)

2 tablespoons salad dressing
(such as Miracle Whip)

2 tablespoons sour cream

1 tablespoon golden raisins,
plumped in hot water for
20 minutes and drained

1 tablespoon honey

1 tablespoon Dijon mustard

2 large eggs, lightly beaten

10 butter crackers (such as Ritz),
roughly crushed

½ pound crabmeat, lump
preferred, picked over for
shells and cartilage

Fred's crab Louis dressing:

1 cup mayonnaise without sugar

¼ cup prepared chili sauce

2 tablespoons minced black
olives

1 tablespoon chopped fresh
chives

2 teaspoons fresh lemon juice

1 teaspoon Worcestershire sauce

1 teaspoon prepared horseradish,
drained

Kosher salt and freshly ground
black pepper to taste

This recipe may seem bizarre to you at first, but among my crab cake taste testers, it got a pretty strong nod of approval. These broiled crab cakes are light and full of great textures—a perfect choice for a fancy luncheon. They are equally good made with blue, Dungeness, or peekytoe crabmeat. Make sure to prepare them the day before you want to serve them.

MAKES ABOUT 8 CRAB CAKES

1. To make the crab cakes, finely chop the slaw by pulsing in a food processor. Combine the slaw, salad dressing, sour cream, raisins, honey, and mustard in a medium-size mixing bowl. Add the eggs and combine. Stir in the crackers until moist. *Fold* in the crabmeat *gently*. Cover and refrigerate for 30 minutes.

2. Form the mixture into 8 cakes, about ⅓ cup each. Place on a baking sheet lined with waxed paper. Cover and refrigerate overnight.

3. To make the dressing, whisk together the mayonnaise, chili sauce, olives, chives, lemon juice, Worcestershire, and horseradish in a small bowl. Season with salt and pepper. Cover and refrigerate for a few hours or overnight. (This will keep refrigerated for about 1 week.)

4. Preheat the broiler. Uncover the cakes and broil until they just begin to brown, about 3 minutes per side. Watch them carefully. Serve warm, with the dressing on the side.

starr's mom's crab croquettes

Starr Laird works at H. Glenwood Evans and Sons Seafood, one of the largest crab buyers in Crisfield, Maryland. When I asked her for her favorite crab recipe, she shared her mother Evelyn Hill's version of an Eastern Shore classic. Cocktail sauce stoked with lots of horseradish is the traditional accompaniment. Almost like a deep-fried crab cake, these are best served with coleslaw. **MAKES 8 CROQUETTES; SERVES 4 TO 6**

2 tablespoons unsalted butter

2 tablespoons all-purpose flour

1 cup whole milk

3 tablespoons prepared yellow mustard

1 tablespoon Worcestershire sauce

2 teaspoons Chesapeake Bay seasoning

1 pound crabmeat, claw meat preferred, picked over for shells and cartilage

3 cups roughly crushed saltines

2 large eggs, lightly beaten

2 tablespoons water

Canola or peanut oil for frying

Cocktail sauce, homemade (see page 38 or 124) or store-bought

1. Melt the butter in a medium-size saucepan over medium heat. When it stops foaming, whisk in the flour until combined. Whisk in the milk and cook, stirring, until thickened, 2 to 3 minutes. Stir in the mustard, Worcestershire, and Bay seasoning. Remove from the heat and let cool slightly. *Fold* the crabmeat *gently* into the sauce. Cover and refrigerate until easy to handle, at least 1 to 2 hours.

2. Using your hands, form the mixture into 8 croquettes shaped almost like a football. Place the saltines in a pie plate. Coat each croquette completely and evenly with the saltines.

3. Combine the eggs and water in a small bowl. Pass each croquette through the mixture and back into the saltines. Place on a baking sheet, cover, and refrigerate for at least 1 hour or up 3 hours.

4. Preheat the oven to 300°F. In an electric skillet, heat 1 inch of oil to 365°F. Fry a few croquettes at a time, turning them as necessary, until golden brown on all sides, about 5 minutes. Drain on paper towels or brown paper bags. (Draining on bags will give you a crisper crust.) Transfer to an ovenproof plate and keep warm in the oven until all the croquettes are fried. Serve hot with cocktail sauce.

THE OLD BLUE CRAB AND OTHER HARD SHELLS

Steaming and boiling crabs is just plain fun. Every region has its own special way of dealing with these hard-shell jewels. In Maryland and much of the Chesapeake Bay region, one must eat crabs steamed, with a red seasoning liberally sprinkled on the shells, making this experience as finger-licking good as anything you can imagine. There are hundreds, maybe thousands, of crab shacks in the region, where a well-versed waitress can walk you through the picking process with ease.

Although boiling is considered a sacrilege by folks in Maryland, a large number of crab aficionados prefer their crabs boiled. In the East, seasonings are added to the boiling liquid, infusing the meat as the crabs cook, while the cook settles back with a beer. On the bayous of the Gulf of Mexico, crawfish, shrimp, sausages, corn, and potatoes are boiled with the crabs for the ultimate one-pot dinner. On the West Coast, Dungeness crabs are usually

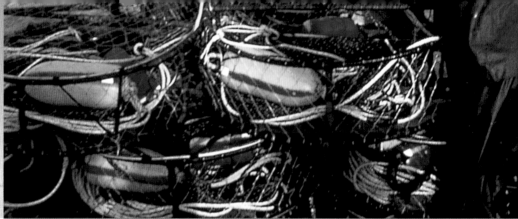

boiled with just salt, and sometimes herbs or spices, added to the water, but the seasonings are always downplayed in favor of the rich crab taste. Chilled cooked Dungeness crabs are for sale everywhere along the Northwest coast.

I am an East Coast fellow, and I'm partial to the blue crabs found from Rhode Island to Florida and in the Gulf of Mexico. Although I may be partial, I'm not stupid. The Pacific Coast Dungeness crab is second to none when it comes to succulence. And any restaurant owner will tell you that an all-you-can-eat Alaskan king crab legs special will have patrons lined up out the door. Florida with no stone crabs? Unthinkable!

Here is a mix of the best ways to cook live hard shells and to use precooked ones. Most of the recipes will work well with any crab readily available in your area. Some of the recipes call for male blue crabs, called jimmies. These are preferred for steaming and boiling because of the amount of meat they contain, but a mix of males and females, or even all females, is fine, although you will probably need to add a few extra crabs to the pot. Don't hesitate to change or alter these recipes to your tastes. Then spread out the newspaper, roll up your sleeves, and get out the mallets: it's time to indulge.

carolina-style
Boiled Blue Crabs

I f you live in or around Maryland or grew up in that area, you can skip this recipe. I once wrote a column about boiled crabs and was taken to task by every person with a tie to Maryland. The rest of my readers loved the idea. Boiling crabs does make the meat softer (which some people consider a negative), but it also infuses lots of flavor directly into the meat. Steaming vs. boiling is a debate that will never be resolved. Try crabs both steamed and boiled, then decide for yourself. As with steaming (see page 118), ice or chill the crabs before introducing them to the pot. **SERVES 4**

12 quarts water

1 medium-size yellow onion, sliced

3 tablespoons distilled white vinegar

3 to 4 tablespoons Chesapeake Bay seasoning, to your taste, plus more for serving

4 bay leaves

1 lemon, halved

Ice as needed to chill the crabs (optional)

24 large live male blue crabs (jimmies)

Melted unsalted butter

Cider vinegar

Cocktail sauce, homemade (see page 38 or 124) or store-bought

1. Pour the water into a 20-quart stockpot and place over high heat. Add the onion, white vinegar, Bay seasoning, bay leaves, and lemon. Bring to a boil and continue to boil for 5 minutes.

2. Meanwhile, ice the crabs in a large tub or cooler, or pop them in the freezer.

3. Add the crabs to the pot, one at a time. They will not be happy about this, so be strong. Once all the crabs are in the pot, cover and set your timer for 20 minutes. Keep an eye on the pot, adjusting the heat so that the liquid doesn't boil over but instead simmers.

4. When the timer goes off, remove the pot from the heat and use large tongs to transfer the crabs to a large roasting pan. (I buy a large aluminum turkey roaster for this.) Let the crabs cool for about 10 minutes, then start picking. Serve with melted butter, cider vinegar, cocktail sauce, and more Chesapeake Bay seasoning so that everyone can satisfy themselves.

CHESAPEAKE BAY STEAMED BLUE CRABS

Two 12-ounce cans or bottles beer, poured out and left to go flat (allow 1 to 2 hours)

1 cup distilled white vinegar

1 cup water

Ice as needed to chill the crabs (optional)

24 large live male crabs (jimmies)

1 cup Chesapeake Bay seasoning, plus more for serving

¼ cup kosher salt

Melted unsalted butter

Cider vinegar

There are as many variations on steamed crabs as there are families in the Chesapeake region, so don't take this recipe as gospel. The process, however, is fairly standard. You will need a good-size steamer pot—at least 12 quarts, even bigger is better—with a tight-fitting lid. The experienced crab steamer also will suggest that you ice the crabs before steaming them. This numbs these feisty critters, making them easier to handle and giving you a better chance of having whole crabs when you finish, rather than crabs that are missing claws and legs. (If you don't ice them, they get very raucous when they hit the steam and will fight with each other like crazy.) You can also put them in your freezer for about 15 minutes. Chilling also helps the seasoning stick. Flat beer is used in this region as a steaming agent. To get it flat, pour it out and let it sit at room temperature for an hour or two. **SERVES 4 NORMAL FOLKS OR 2 VERY HUNGRY ONES**

1. Pour the beer, white vinegar, and water into a steamer pot with a rack fitted high enough to clear the liquid. Cover and bring to a boil.

2. Meanwhile, ice the crabs in a big tub or cooler, or pop them in the freezer. Stir the Bay seasoning and salt together in a small bowl.

3. When the liquid has reached a full boil, place a layer of crabs in the pot. Sprinkle liberally with the seasoning mixture. Work quickly so as not to lose too much heat. Continue layering and seasoning until all the crabs are in the pot and all the seasoning is used. Cover, reduce the heat to medium-high, and steam for exactly 25 minutes. (Don't ask, just do it.)

4. Serve hot with melted butter, cider vinegar, and more Bay seasoning. Any leftovers (which I doubt you'll have) can be refrigerated for a day or so.

Louisiana crab boil

12 quarts water

1 cup kosher salt

2 packages dry crab and shrimp boil

¼ cup liquid crab and shrimp boil

2 tablespoons Creole seasoning

2 tablespoons hot pepper sauce

12 small to medium-size new red potatoes

3 large yellow onions, unpeeled and quartered

2 lemons, halved

1 head garlic, halved crosswise to expose as much of the cloves as possible

Ice as needed to chill the crabs (optional)

24 to 30 large live male blue crabs (jimmies)

¾ pound andouille or other spicy sausages

6 ears fresh corn, husked and broken in half

along the northern Gulf coast, particularly in Louisiana, a crab boil takes on a different look. The crabs team up with potatoes, corn, smoked sausages, and most likely shrimp or crawfish—a one-pot meal, so to speak. This recipe has 2 ingredients you may not be familiar with: packaged dry crab and shrimp boil, and liquid crab and shrimp boil. These 2 products are standard seasonings on the Gulf Coast and in other coastal areas, just as Chesapeake Bay seasoning is in the Chesapeake. The packaged dry seasoning looks a lot like pickling spices and actually does include many of the same ingredients, such as bay leaves, mustard seeds, coriander seeds, black peppercorns, and allspice berries. It is sold in a steeping bag so that the spices can be easily removed from the pot, or just loose in a box that weighs around 3.5 ounces. Liquid boil is a highly concentrated liquid version of the dry. I like using both so that I get a well-rounded, robust cooking liquid. Both of these seasonings are widely available in supermarkets. Note that this boil is a little spicier than some of the others, and it's perfect when paired with coleslaw. **SERVES 4 TO 6**

1. Pour the water into a steamer pot and add the salt, dry boil, liquid boil, Creole seasoning, hot pepper sauce, potatoes, onions, lemons, and garlic. Bring to a boil, cover, reduce the heat to medium, and simmer for 20 minutes.

2. Meanwhile, ice the crabs in a large tub or cooler, or pop them in the freezer.

3. Add the sausages, corn, and crabs to the pot, pushing and stirring

everything around. Ratchet the heat up to high, return to a boil, cover, and boil for 5 minutes. Turn off the heat and let stand for 15 to 30 minutes. The longer it steeps, the spicier everything will be. Drain and serve.

Variation: To include shrimp or crawfish in this boil, add them in step 3 after the liquid has come back to a full boil, not when you add the crabs.

carroll leggett's mother's coleslaw

Carroll Leggett is an old-time backroom politics guy in North Carolina. He gleaned most of his cooking chops from helping his mother in the kitchen while growing up in Harnett County, North Carolina. I like this coleslaw recipe for a couple of reasons. First, the kale gives the slaw some visual character. Second, it pairs beautifully with crab cakes, soft-shell crabs, steamed crabs, and crab casseroles. Carroll likes to make it 4 or 5 hours in advance. Refrigerate the cabbage and kale a few hours before chopping them so they will be crisp. **SERVES 8**

4 cups lightly packed cored and roughly chopped cabbage

¼ cup chopped sweet gherkins

3 tablespoons chopped yellow onion

2 tablespoons chopped kale (for color)

2 teaspoons sweet gherkin juice

¼ teaspoon kosher salt

⅛ teaspoon white pepper

¼ teaspoon celery seeds

½ teaspoon sugar

½ teaspoon Dijon mustard

½ cup mayonnaise

Toss the cabbage, gherkins, onion, and kale together in a large mixing bowl. Add the gherkin juice, salt, pepper, celery seeds, and sugar and toss well to coat. Add the mustard and mayonnaise and mix thoroughly to coat everything well. Cover with plastic wrap and refrigerate for 2 to 4 hours. Stir well before serving.

crab feeds, feasts, and boils

americans love to get together to enjoy the bounty of their regions, whether it be devouring a New England clambake, picking a pig in North Carolina, smoking a brisket in Texas, or cracking and eating crabs. Used as fundraisers for fire departments, churches, and politicians or just plain fun entertaining for a bunch of friends and family, this kind of eating is a pure delight. No pretense, no social graces to worry about, just long tables of excited folks hungry for crab. I urge you never to pass up an invite to a crab-eating event. One of my most memorable meals was a crab feed at the Knights of Columbus Hall in Mendocino, California. Here's what to expect from crab feasts across the country and a guide for hosting one at home.

Along the Northwest coast, these events are known as crab feeds. They are fairly straightforward affairs, focused on the prized Dungeness crab. The menu is simple: boatloads of cooked and cracked Dungeness, sometimes chilled, other times warmed slightly in an herb-infused broth, and occasionally served in a warm, spicy broth. In Washington State,

clam chowder is usually on the menu, but that can fill you up before the main event begins. A chopped salad with Italian dressing seems to be a recurring theme, but coleslaw also shows up at many feeds. Sourdough or garlic bread completes the feed. Since this same general area produces some of America's best wines, folks bring their favorites and always share. Microbrew beers are preferred. What really tickled me in Mendocino was all the sauce fixings people brought. It seemed as if every family or group had their own favorite sauce (or sauces) for crab dipping, and this just added to the merry chaos. Plenty of warm melted butter is a must. One warning: don't ever swipe picked crabmeat from a fellow diner—it's simply not done.

For a West Coast–style feed at your house, plan on 1 to 2 crabs per person. Cover the tables with newspaper for easy cleanup. Supply bibs for your guests and have some "community" crackers and mallets handy. Put out several rolls of paper towels—you don't need to bother with napkins. See page 126 for basic cooking instructions. Serve the crabs in huge bowls spread out among your

guest pickers. Serve with a chopped salad, bread, melted butter, and Fred's Crab Louis Dressing (page 112). Other dishes are up to you, but wine and beer will be expected. Have everyone check their manners at the door and enjoy.

On the East Coast, a crab *feed* becomes a crab *feast*, and on the Chesapeake Bay, a feast is viewed as an art form. There, a crab feast means steamed crabs seasoned with somebody's secret crab spice blend, which will turn your fingers reddish orange no matter how much you lick them. The sides served with the crabs vary. In the northern Chesapeake and around Annapolis, a "boil" is usually served—a mixture of smoked sausages, shrimp, potatoes, and corn cooked in a highly seasoned broth. Occasionally, crab cakes are served, but that's infrequent. Since the prime crab season coincides with a wealth of garden vegetables ready for picking, sliced ripe tomatoes and sweet corn on the cob are a given. Coleslaw, potato salad, or a vegetable salad rounds out the feast. Dessert usually consists of fresh fruit, especially watermelon. The drink of choice is beer, and lots of it.

To do an East Coast feast at home, plan on at least 6 jimmies per person. Follow the steaming instructions on page 118. Cover the tables with newspaper and have bibs, mallets, and crackers on hand. Provide loads of paper towels instead of napkins; wet wipes or damp cloths also are helpful. You will want to have extra crab spice, cider vinegar, and melted butter on the table for serving with the crabs. Keep the beer good and cold for the adults, and serve ginger ale, or ginger ale mixed with fruit juice, for the kids. If you would rather boil the crabs, see page 117, but everything else is the same.

On the Gulf Coast, folks are into one-pot cooking. A crab boil is the norm in this area. Not only will there be crabs in the pot, but there will also be potatoes, corn, smoked sausages, peppers (both hot and sweet), shrimp, and/or crawfish. Everything is cooked together, with different ingredients being added at different times (see page 120), then drained and dumped onto newspaper-covered tables. A fun free-for-all ensues. Purists serve only French bread; others add coleslaw. And again, there's beer, beer, and more beer.

6 quarts water

2 lemons, sliced

1 large sweet onion, sliced

½ cup Chesapeake Bay seasoning

⅓ cup kosher salt

Ice as needed to chill the crabs (optional)

24 large live male blue crabs (jimmies)

Melted unsalted butter

Cocktail sauce, homemade (see page 38 or below) or store-bought

Stone crabs get all the glory in Florida, but a good portion of blue crabs come from the waters around this peninsula, too. This is a slightly different way to season boiled crabs. **SERVES 4 TO 6**

1. Pour the water into a large stockpot or steamer pot and bring to a boil over high heat. Place the lemons, onion, and Bay seasoning in the center of a 12-inch square of cheesecloth. Tie up into a bundle and add to the water along with the salt. Reduce the heat to medium and simmer for about 10 minutes.

2. Ice the crabs in a large tub or cooler, or pop them in the freezer.

3. Bring the liquid back to a full boil, then plunge the crabs into the liquid. Cover, reduce the heat slightly, and cook for 20 minutes. Drain and serve with melted butter and cocktail sauce.

cocktail sauce al's way

1 cup ketchup

1 tablespoon prepared horseradish, drained

Squirt of fresh lemon juice (optional)

Dash of Worcestershire sauce (optional)

My "second dad," Al Haskins, always told me, "A good cocktail sauce should have enough horseradish in it to make you sweat right under your eyes." This cocktail sauce is not that hot; adjust it up or down to accommodate your heat tolerance. A nice way to do cocktail sauce is to put out the ketchup, horseradish, lemon wedges, and a bottle of Worcestershire sauce and let everybody make their own. **MAKES ABOUT 1¼ CUPS**

Mix the ingredients together in a small bowl. Cover and refrigerate overnight. Serve chilled. This will keep for 1 week, if it lasts that long.

crab "doublers"

The first time I heard of this dish was at the Crab Claw Restaurant in St. Michaels, Maryland. As I considered ordering it, I asked my waitress to describe this crab variation. "It's like a prehistoric monster on a plate," she said with a straight face. Well, I had to see what that was about, and she was right—a monster crab. You really get 3 crab experiences with this recipe: steamed crab, a crab cake, and fried crab. Make one of these, and you'll understand the waitress's comment. **SERVES 6**

1. To make the batter, stir together the baking mix, Bay seasoning, salt, pepper, Worcestershire, hot pepper sauce, and eggs in a medium-size mixing bowl. Whisk in the milk and set aside.

2. To make the filling, combine the crabmeat, egg white, bread crumbs, and Bay seasoning together in another medium-size mixing bowl and set aside.

3. Add oil to a deep fryer according to the manufacturer's instructions and heat to 375°F.

4. Stuff the cavity of each steamed crab with filling. Dip the filled crabs one at a time into the batter. (If the batter is too thick, thin it with milk until it coats the crab.) Place 1 or 2 in the fryer and cook until golden brown, 8 to 10 minutes, turning once. Drain on paper towels or brown paper bags. (Draining on bags will give you a crisper crust.) Repeat with remaining crabs. Serve immediately with tartar sauce or cocktail sauce.

Batter:

1 cup baking mix (such as Bisquick) or pancake flour

1 teaspoon Chesapeake Bay seasoning

1 teaspoon kosher salt

1 teaspoon freshly ground black pepper

1 teaspoon Worcestershire sauce

½ teaspoon hot pepper sauce

2 large eggs, lightly beaten

One 5-ounce can evaporated milk, or more if needed to keep the batter loose

Filling:

1 pound crabmeat, backfin or special preferred, picked over for shells and cartilage

1 large egg white, lightly beaten

¼ cup fresh bread crumbs

½ teaspoon Chesapeake Bay seasoning

Canola or peanut oil for frying

6 live blue crabs, steamed (see page 118), innards and leathery gray gills discarded, and top shell removed but otherwise intact

Tartar sauce or cocktail sauce, homemade (see page 101, 124, or 38) or store-bought

west coast Dungeness crab Boil

12 quarts water

Ice as needed to chill the crabs (optional)

4 live Dungeness crabs (about 2 pounds each)

1½ cups kosher salt

Melted unsalted butter

Lemon wedges

Cocktail sauce, homemade (page 38 or 124) or store-bought

Fred's Crab Louis Dressing (page 112)

Few of us will ever be lucky enough to have access to live Dungeness crabs. If you live along the northern coastal regions of California, Oregon, or Washington, I envy you the ability to get fresh live Dungeness crabs during the fall and winter months.

Unlike blue crabs, where the seasoning is so important in the boiling or steaming, little is done to Dungeness crabs other than adding salt to the water. Duncan Thomson, who cooks Dungeness crabs in an open-air rig at North Noyo Harbor near Fort Bragg, California, has a cut-and-dried recipe: 1 pound of salt for every 10 pounds of crab, boil for 25 minutes. Nothing could be simpler. What follows is a version for the home cook.

SERVES 4 TO 6

1. Pour the water into a large steamer pot and bring to a boil over high heat.

2. Meanwhile, ice the crabs in a tub or cooler, or pop them in the freezer.

3. Add the salt to the water, stirring to dissolve. Add the crabs, shell side down, one at a time. Cover the pot and reduce the heat to medium. Cook until the crabs are orange-red and are floating, 18 to 25 minutes.

4. Serve with melted butter, lemon wedges, cocktail sauce, and crab Louis dressing.

Variation: You also can cook cleaned raw crab portions this way. Just decrease your cooking time to 15 minutes. If you want to serve the crab chilled, ice the portions down while they are still warm.

Dungeness Crabs in Black Bean Sauce

The Chinese treasure crabs, and one of their best preparations is to stir-fry them with fermented black beans. You can use almost any pre-cooked crab in its shell in this recipe, but Dungeness is especially delicious. This is really messy to eat but well worth the cleanup. Like any Asian stir-fry, have all your ingredients ready and close by, because the cooking goes very fast. You can find the fermented black beans and rice vinegar in the Asian foods section of most large supermarkets. **SERVES 4**

1. Heat the oil in a wok or large, heavy skillet over high heat. When almost smoking, add the garlic and ginger and stir-fry for 30 seconds. Add the scallions and stir-fry for 30 seconds. Stir in the black beans, vinegar, chicken broth, tamari, and sugar and cook, stirring, for about 2 minutes. Add the crab, reduce the heat to a simmer, cover, and cook for 2 minutes.

2. In a small bowl, mix together the water and cornstarch to make a slurry.

3. Uncover the wok and transfer the crab to a plate. Increase the heat to high and add the slurry, stirring until the liquid has thickened. Return the crab to the wok and stir quickly to coat with sauce. Serve immediately.

¼ cup peanut or canola oil

2 tablespoons finely chopped garlic

2 tablespoons peeled and finely minced fresh ginger

4 scallions (white and green parts), sliced on the diagonal

⅓ cup fermented black beans in garlic sauce

¼ cup seasoned rice vinegar

¼ cup reduced-sodium chicken broth

1½ tablespoons tamari or other low-sodium soy sauce

1 tablespoon sugar

2 precooked Dungeness crabs (about 2 pounds each), cleaned and portioned (see page 19)

2 tablespoons water

1 teaspoon cornstarch

SPICY DUNGENESS CRAB BOIL

4 quarts water or equal parts water and beer, poured out and left to go flat (allow 1 to 2 hours)

2 tablespoons yellow mustard seeds

2 teaspoons red pepper flakes

3 bay leaves

4 precooked Dungeness crabs (about 2 pounds each), cleaned and portioned (see page 19)

This crab boil may not be spicy compared to those on the Atlantic and Gulf coasts, but it definitely jacks up the flavor of these sweet Dungeness crabs. Pour a little of the broth over the crabs as you serve them. If you have live crabs, just boil them longer. **SERVES 4 TO 6**

1. Bring the water to a boil in a large stockpot. Add the mustard seeds, red pepper flakes, and bay leaves. Reduce the heat to a simmer and cook for 10 minutes.

2. Add the crab portions and cook for at least 3 minutes but no more than 5 minutes. Serve with a little of the broth and lots of napkins.

---

beach bourbon slush

My annual summer beach vacation would not be complete without a batch of this wonderful concoction in the freezer at the condo. A glass of this marvelous elixir, and a plate of crab—well, it's pretty close to nirvana. **THE NUMBER OF SERVINGS DEPENDS ON WHO'S DRINKING**

2 cups strong brewed tea

5 cups water

2 cups Black Label Jack Daniel's

¼ cup sugar

One 12-ounce can frozen lemonade concentrate, defrosted

One 6-ounce can frozen orange juice concentrate, defrosted

One 2-quart bottle ginger ale

1. In a large metal bowl (that will fit in your freezer), combine all the ingredients except the ginger ale. Place the bowl in the freezer and every couple of hours or so, stir the mixture, until it is frozen.

2. To serve, scrape the icy mixture with a spoon and fill a highball glass about two-thirds full with it. Top with ginger ale, sit back, and enjoy.

jackie's marinated Dungeness crabs

I was lucky to meet Frank Bertoni, who has been fishing and crabbing the north coast of California for decades. He and his wife, Jackie, entertained me for hours with fishing tales and stories of being married in this business. They are great folks, and I was honored when Jackie agreed to share this recipe with me. Its Italian overtones bring out the rich flavor of Dungeness crab. This recipe also works well with other cooked crabs in the shell. Be sure to serve some crusty bread to sop up the juices.

SERVES 4 TO 6

1. Combine all the ingredients except the bread in a large mixing bowl, making sure the crab pieces are well covered with marinade. Cover with plastic wrap and refrigerate overnight or up to 2 days. Every time you think about it, give the crab a stir.

2. Serve cold with some of the marinade and lots of crusty bread.

4 to 6 precooked Dungeness crabs (about 2 pounds each), cleaned and portioned (see page 19)

1 head garlic, cloves separated and peeled

1 cup chopped fresh Italian parsley leaves

1 cup good-quality extra virgin olive oil

¼ to ⅓ cup balsamic vinegar, to your taste

2 teaspoons red pepper flakes

About 1 teaspoon prepared yellow mustard, to your taste

Crusty bread

alaskan king or snow crab legs

King and snow crabs come to market as cooked legs, and Americans absolutely love them. Buy king and snow crabs that are still frozen rather than thawed. To defrost them, put them in a large baking pan (they release lots of liquid) and refrigerate overnight. Most legs come already cracked, but if they are not, tap them with the back of a kitchen knife to crack them lightly. This allows any flavorings to seep in and makes them easier to eat. You can steam, grill, bake, or broil crab legs. **TWO POUNDS OF CRAB LEGS WILL FEED 2 TO 3 PEOPLE**

To Steam: Place a steaming rack in a large pot. Add enough water to just touch the bottom of the rack. If you wish, add garlic, lemongrass, sliced fresh ginger, or herbs to the water. Cover the pot and bring to a boil over high heat. Add the legs, cover, and reduce the heat slightly. Steam for about 5 minutes. Serve with melted butter, cocktail sauce, or a light vinaigrette.

To Grill: Brush the legs with olive oil or melted butter. Place them meat (or cracked) side up on a medium-hot grill. Grill until hot, 3 to 5 minutes. Serve with melted butter, an Asian dipping sauce, lemon wedges, or cocktail sauce. The smoky flavor that grilling imparts is irresistible.

To Bake: Preheat the oven to 350°F. Place the legs in a single layer in a roasting pan. Bake until hot, 6 to 8 minutes. Serve with melted butter, vinaigrette, lemon wedges, or cocktail sauce.

To Broil: Preheat the broiler. Brush the legs with melted butter or olive oil and season with salt and pepper, if you wish. Place in a single layer on a broiling pan and broil until hot, 3 to 4 minutes. Serve with melted butter, lemon wedges, a fruity olive oil, or cocktail sauce.

stone crab claws, warm and cold

Stone crab claws are Florida's gift to the world, and thanks to overnight delivery, we don't have to be in Florida to enjoy them. Stone crabs are regularly harvested from the Cedar Keys along the Gulf coast, south through the Florida Keys, then north to Miami and Hollywood. Although most purists prefer their claws cold, warming them slightly does them no harm, and many folks in this region like them that way. I found that I do, too. Here's how to prepare them both ways. **20 TO 30 MEDIUM-SIZE CLAWS WILL FEED ABOUT 4 PEOPLE**

Warm Stone Crab Claws: Place the claws in a large Dutch oven and cover with warm tap water. Slowly bring to a boil over medium heat, then drain immediately. Serve with melted butter and lemon wedges.

Cold Stone Crab Claws: Take the claws out of the refrigerator and serve with mustard sauce (recipes follow).

horseradish-mustard sauce

1 cup mayonnaise

¼ cup prepared yellow mustard

¼ cup prepared horseradish, drained

1 to 2 teaspoons fresh lime or lemon juice, to your taste

Dash of hot pepper sauce

Mustard sauce is expected when serving stone crab claws, and my research turned up some variations on the theme. Along the Gulf coast of Florida, a horseradish and mustard combo seems to prevail. This is an excellent example that takes no time to prepare and is truly sublime. **MAKES ABOUT 1½ CUPS**

Mix the mayonnaise, mustard, horseradish, 1 teaspoon of the juice, and the hot pepper sauce together in a small mixing bowl. Taste and add the remaining juice, if desired. Refrigerate until ready to serve.

almost Like joe's mustard sauce

The temple of stone crabs is Miami's famous Joe's Stone Crab Restaurant. Founded by Joe Weiss in 1913, this restaurant is credited with putting stone crabs on the map in the culinary world and also lays claim to devising the best way to cook and serve stone crab claws, which Joe's believes is chilled. Joe's mustard sauce is almost as well known as its crabs. The twist to Joe's sauce is the addition of steak sauce. This is my version, which also pairs nicely with other crab legs, as well as with lump crabmeat.

MAKES ABOUT 1 CUP

1 cup mayonnaise

2 teaspoons dry mustard

2 teaspoons Worcestershire sauce

1 teaspoon steak sauce

Kosher salt to taste

Milk or heavy cream for thinning (optional)

Mix together the mayonnaise, mustard, Worcestershire, and steak sauce in a small bowl. Season with salt, then thin to your desired consistency, if necessary. Refrigerate until ready to serve.

THE SUBLIME SOFT SHELLS

For a long time, soft-shell crabs were the secret of the East Coast. A soft-shell crab, or soft, as it is referred to along the Chesapeake Bay, is simply a blue crab that has shed its hard shell, or molted, allowing the crab to grow. An average blue crab might molt 20 or more times during its life. All crabs molt, but only the blue crab has been marketed successfully in this condition, to the delight of crab lovers everywhere.

Actually, "marketed successfully" is an understatement—wildly successful is more appropriate. When soft-shell season opens in late March in Florida, chefs start to salivate. New York City has its own peculiar competition, as top restaurants in the city vie to be the first to have soft shells on their menu. The honor usually merits a mention in the *New York Times* and other local newspapers and magazines. This scene is repeated in major cities around the country. As the waters of the Atlantic warm up in May and into the summer, soft shells are abundant. Crisfield, Maryland, has developed a major industry around softs, with the John T. Handy Company being the largest producer and supplier of soft shells anywhere.

Soft-shell crabs are worked from *floats*, tanks in which the water temperature and other factors are carefully controlled. *Peelers*, crabs that are beginning to molt, are placed in the floats and care-

fully monitored 24 hours a day. Experienced human eyes know exactly when to remove the crabs from the tanks. If left even a few hours too long in the water, the crabs will start to harden. It is demanding work, and this is an extremely oversimplified version of what actually goes on, but I hope you understand that getting soft-shell crabs to market is no piece of cake.

Most of this information is included in the basics chapter, but bears repeating here. Soft shells are sold live and frozen. If you're buying them live, they need to really be alive. I know that sounds silly, but sometimes it's hard to tell. Look for bubbles around the face and some movement, although they are very docile at this stage. See page 30 for instructions on how to clean, or dress, live soft shells. Plan on cooking them the day you buy them.

This chapter has it all for the soft-shell lover—sophisticated Asian flavors, fancy Southern-style softs, and down-home cornmeal-fried morsels. While the rest of us clamor over soft shells as a gourmet treat, to people on the Chesapeake, soft shells are just regular old food. A fried soft-shell crab sandwich seems to be the favorite among the locals—nothing more than two slices of white bread painted with some mayonnaise, a slice or two of a summer-ripe beefsteak tomato, and a pan-fried soft shell. Man, that's good eating.

basic simple soft-shell crabs

Cooking soft-shell crabs spooks some people, but it really should not. Here are a few general rules.

Use clarified butter, equal parts butter and oil, or just oil or shortening to cook the crabs. If you try to sauté soft crabs in butter alone at the heat you will need, the butter will smoke and burn quickly, leaving you with a mess. I like the butter and oil combination because you get the flavor of the butter and the higher smoking point of the oil. I'm also too lazy to clarify butter. Crabs are creatures of the water and will always retain some moisture. Get them as dry as you can, but realize that they probably will "spit" when they make contact with the hot fat. In other words, wear an apron. Crabs cook very quickly and become dry and nasty if you overcook them. Usually a couple of minutes per side is enough. Look for nice browning and a reddish hue, then get them out of the pan. **SERVES 4**

2 cups all-purpose flour

1 tablespoon Chesapeake Bay seasoning

4 to 8 hotel or prime soft-shell crabs (depending on their size and your hunger), dressed (see page 30)

Kosher salt and freshly ground black pepper to taste

¼ cup (½ stick) unsalted butter

¼ cup canola or peanut oil

1 lemon, cut into wedges

1. Combine the flour and Bay seasoning in a pie plate. Pat the crabs dry, then sprinkle with salt and pepper. Dredge the crabs with the flour mixture, covering all parts and shaking off any excess.

2. Heat 2 tablespoons each of the butter and oil together in a large skillet over medium-high heat. *Take care in the next step, as the crabs hold moisture and tend to "spit" when they hit the hot fat.* When the butter has melted and the fat is very hot, add a couple of the crabs, top shell down. Reduce the heat a bit and cook for about 3 minutes, then turn and cook another 3 minutes. Using tongs, remove the crabs from the hot oil and drain on paper towels or brown paper bags. (Draining on bags will give you a crisper crust.) Repeat with the remaining crabs, adding the remaining 2 tablespoons butter and 2 tablespoons oil as needed.

3. Serve as fast as you can, with lemon wedges.

Beer-Battered Soft-Shell Crabs

1¼ cups all-purpose flour,
plus ¼ cup for dredging

2 teaspoons kosher salt

½ teaspoon baking powder

1 teaspoon paprika

½ teaspoon Chesapeake Bay
seasoning

One 12-ounce can or bottle beer,
poured out and left to go flat
(allow 1 to 2 hours)

8 hotel or prime soft-shell crabs,
dressed (see page 30)

Vegetable oil for frying

Tartar sauce, homemade (see
page 101) or store-bought

Lemon wedges

Cider vinegar

With tongue in cheek, I like to call beer-battered crabs redneck tempura. The chemistry behind both is similar, as is their look, but there's something about that hint of beer that makes beer-battered crabs special. Since beer is the beverage of choice at any official crab feast (okay, Chardonnay in California), a beer batter is a perfect choice for soft-shell crabs. Using flat beer does away with any metallic flavor and smoothes the taste. **SERVES 4 TO 6**

1. Sift together the 1¼ cups flour, salt, baking powder, paprika, and Bay seasoning in a large mixing bowl. Slowly whisk in the beer to make a smooth batter. Cover and let sit at room temperature for 1 to 2 hours. The batter will thicken.

2. Lightly dredge the soft shells with the remaining ¼ cup flour, gently shaking off any excess. Heat about 1 inch of oil in a large, deep skillet or deep fryer until it shimmers but before it starts to smoke, about 375°F. Dip the crabs one at a time into the batter to coat evenly, letting the excess drip off. *Take care in the next step, as the crabs hold moisture and tend to "spit" when they hit the hot oil.* Slip the crabs into the oil and fry until golden brown, 3 to 5 minutes. Fry only a few at a time so the temperature of the oil stays constant. Using tongs, transfer the crabs to paper towels or brown paper bags to drain. (Draining on bags will give you a crisper crust.)

3. Serve immediately with tartar sauce, lemon wedges, and vinegar.

macadamia nut–crusted soft-shell crabs

I was inspired to develop this recipe after having had my fill of pecan-crusted soft shells in so many restaurants. You can substitute pecans here and have an amazing dish, but why not go one better? **SERVES 4**

1. Sift the 1½ cups flour, baking powder, Bay seasoning, and pepper into a large mixing bowl. Slowly whisk in the water to make a smooth batter. Cover and let sit at room temperature for 1 hour, then stir in the nuts.

2. Heat 1 inch of oil in a large, deep skillet over medium-high heat until it shimmers but doesn't smoke, about 375°F. Preheat the oven to 200°F.

3. Put the remaining ¼ cup flour in a pie plate and dredge the crabs one at a time, tapping off any excess. Dip each crab into the batter, letting any excess drip off. *Take care in the next step, as the crabs hold moisture and tend to "spit" when they hit the hot oil.* Slip 2 to 3 crabs at a time into the oil and cook until golden, 3 to 4 minutes per side. Using tongs, transfer the crabs to paper towels or brown paper bags to drain. (Draining on bags will give you a crisper crust.) Transfer to an ovenproof plate and keep warm in the oven.

4. When all the crabs are cooked, make the sauce. Pour the oil out of the skillet and return the skillet to medium heat. Carefully add the bourbon and scrape the bottom of the pan, bringing up any browned bits left from the crabs. Reduce the heat to low and add the lemon juice. Whisk in the butter one piece at a time until it is all incorporated. Remove from the heat and stir in the parsley.

5. Place 2 crabs on each dinner plate and divide the sauce among the plates, pouring it over the crabs. Serve at once.

1½ cups all-purpose flour, plus ¼ cup for dredging

½ teaspoon baking powder

1 teaspoon Chesapeake Bay seasoning

½ teaspoon freshly ground black pepper

¾ cup cold water

½ cup finely chopped macadamia nuts

Canola or peanut oil for frying

8 hotel or prime soft-shell crabs, dressed (see page 30)

Bourbon-lemon sauce:

¼ cup bourbon

¼ cup fresh lemon juice

½ cup (1 stick) unsalted butter, cut into small pieces

2 tablespoons chopped fresh Italian parsley leaves

elaine's on franklin's southern fried crabs with creamy slaw

elaine's on Franklin in Chapel Hill, North Carolina, has an able and talented chef/owner by the name of Bret Jennings. Bret loves world cuisines and has studied in some of the top Paris eateries. Although his menu at Elaine's draws on the best flavors from around the world, he is a purist when it comes to using regional foodstuffs. "Soft-shell crabs are a wonderful seasonal treat indigenous to the southeastern coastal states, and we try and take advantage of these guys in their peak season," Bret says. This is one of my favorite soft-shell crab dishes, and it's Southern to the bone. **SERVES 3**

1. To make the aioli, combine the egg yolks, vinegar, lemon juice, garlic, salt, and Tabasco in a food processor or blender. With the machine running, slowly drizzle in the oil through the feed tube, processing until the mixture thickens. Adjust the lemon juice, salt, and Tabasco to your taste. Set aside ½ cup of the aioli for the slaw dressing. Place the rest of it in a squeeze tube to use as a garnish. This dressing will keep in the refrigerator for 3 to 4 days.

2. To make the slaw dressing, combine all the ingredients in a small mixing bowl.

3. To make the slaw, combine the cabbage, carrot, onion, bell peppers, garlic, and salt in a large mixing bowl. Add the dressing and toss to combine and coat well. Let sit at room temperature for 30 minutes. Add the parsley, oregano, and arugula and toss.

Tabasco aioli:

2 very fresh large egg yolks (see Note on page 108)

1 tablespoon cider vinegar

1 tablespoon fresh lemon juice

1½ teaspoons finely minced garlic

1 teaspoon kosher salt

2 tablespoons Tabasco sauce

1 cup olive oil

Slaw dressing:

½ cup Tabasco aioli

2 tablespoons cider vinegar

Pinch of sugar

1 tablespoon celery seeds

Slaw:

1 small head cabbage, cored and sliced as thinly as possible

1 medium-size carrot, cut into matchsticks

½ medium-size red onion, thinly sliced

1 medium-size red bell pepper, seeded and cut into matchsticks

1 medium-size yellow bell pepper, seeded and cut into matchsticks

1 clove garlic, finely minced

Kosher salt to taste

1 tablespoon chopped fresh Italian parsley leaves

1 tablespoon chopped fresh
   oregano leaves

½ pound baby arugula or
   spinach, washed well and
   patted dry

Crabs:

3 cups corn oil

3 cups yellow cornmeal

½ cup all-purpose flour

1 tablespoon kosher salt

1 teaspoon cayenne pepper

6 hotel or prime soft-shell crabs

1 cup buttermilk

1 bunch scallions (white and
   green parts), thinly sliced,
   for garnish

4. Meanwhile, prepare the crabs. Heat the oil in a large, deep cast-iron skillet or other heavy pot until it shimmers but hasn't started to smoke, about 375°F. Combine the cornmeal, flour, salt, and cayenne in a baking dish or other large container. Clean the crabs by removing the gills, tails, and faces just before cooking (see page 30). (Bret believes that cleaning them right before cooking improves their flavor.) Dip the crabs into the buttermilk, then dredge them with the cornmeal mixture. *Take care in the next step, as the crabs hold moisture and tend to "spit" when they hit the hot oil.* Carefully place the crabs top side down in the oil. Fry until browned, about 3 minutes. Turn over and fry for 30 seconds. Using tongs, transfer the crabs to paper towels or brown paper bags to drain. (Draining on bags will give you a crisper crust.)

5. Divide the slaw among 3 serving plates, place 2 crabs on each plate, and drizzle with the aioli in the squeeze tube. Garnish with the scallions and serve at once.

---

how 'bout a po' boy?

the po' boy, or poor boy, is the signature sandwich of New Orleans and was developed during a streetcar workers strike in 1914 to feed the "poor boys" who were out of work. There are many variations on a po' boy, but the most famous are those made with fried seafood, especially oysters. During soft-shell season, you will find many a soft-shell po' boy, and it is one hell of a sandwich. Simply split a French roll lengthwise, spread a heavy layer of homemade tartar sauce (see page 101) on both sides of the roll, and fill it up with 2 or 3 pan-fried soft shells. If you want it "dressed," add some tomato slices and lettuce.

CRAB-STUFFED SOFT-SHELL CRAB SUPREME

This dish is 2 treats in 1: a crispy soft-shell crab and a crab cake, both covered with a decadent sauce. Folks around the Chesapeake sometimes call this preparation doublers (see page 125 for another doubler recipe). Save this dish for a celebration. **SERVES 6**

1. Preheat the oven to 325°F. Combine the flour and Bay seasoning in a pie plate. Dredge the crabs with the mixture, shaking off any excess.

2. Heat the butter and oil in a large skillet over medium-high heat until the butter stops foaming. *Take care in the next step, as the crabs hold moisture and tend to "spit" when they hit the hot fat.* Pan-fry the crabs several at a time until golden brown, about 3 minutes per side. Using tongs, transfer the crabs to paper towels or brown paper bags to drain. (Draining on bags will give you a crisper crust.)

3. Before you make the stuffing, make sure that you have picked over the crabmeat meticulously. Nothing spoils this dish like biting down on a piece of shell. Combine the bell pepper, onion, mustard, garlic powder, Bay seasoning, lemon juice, white pepper, sour cream, saltines, and flour in a large mixing bowl. In another large mixing bowl, beat the egg whites with an electric mixer until soft peaks form, then fold them into the bell pepper mixture. Carefully fold in the crabmeat, trying not to break up any large pieces. Fill the soft-shell crabs with the stuffing. Place the crabs in a single layer in 2 baking dishes.

4. To make the sauce, combine all the ingredients in a medium-size mixing bowl. Pour over the stuffed crabs and bake until golden brown, about 30 minutes. Serve hot.

Crabs:

1 cup all-purpose flour

1 teaspoon Chesapeake Bay seasoning

6 hotel or prime soft-shell crabs, dressed (see page 30)

2 tablespoons unsalted butter

1 tablespoon canola oil

Stuffing:

1 pound crabmeat, backfin preferred, picked over for shells and cartilage

2 teaspoons seeded and finely diced green bell pepper

1 teaspoon finely diced yellow onion

2 teaspoons Dijon mustard

¼ teaspoon garlic powder

½ teaspoon Chesapeake Bay seasoning

1 teaspoon fresh lemon juice

½ teaspoon white pepper

3 tablespoons sour cream

8 saltines, roughly crushed

4 teaspoons all-purpose flour

4 large egg whites

Sauce:

6 large eggs, lightly beaten

½ cup sour cream

1 teaspoon fresh lemon juice

1 teaspoon Chesapeake Bay seasoning

¼ teaspoon garlic powder

1 teaspoon paprika

SOFT-SHELL CRABS WITH CORN SAUCE

4 cups water

2 cups fresh corn kernels

3 tablespoons half-and-half

4 teaspoons olive oil

½ cup roughly chopped red onion

½ cup chopped roasted red bell
pepper (jarred is fine)

Kosher salt and freshly ground
black pepper to taste

4 hotel or prime soft-shell crabs,
dressed (see page 30)

1 lemon, cut into wedges

The ultimate summer treat is soft-shell crabs and corn. The lush sweetness of both combine for a compelling taste triumph. Pair this with a ripe tomato salad, and summer will be on your table. **SERVES 2**

1. Bring the water to a boil in a medium-size saucepan. Add the corn and cook for 2 minutes. Drain and transfer to a food processor or blender. Add the half-and-half and process until smooth. Set aside.

2. Heat 2 teaspoons of the oil in a medium-size nonstick skillet over medium heat. Add the onion and cook until it softens and just begins to brown, about 10 minutes. Add the corn puree and roasted pepper and heat through. Season with salt and pepper. Remove from the heat and cover to keep warm.

3. Pat the crabs dry. Heat the remaining 2 teaspoons oil in a large skillet over high heat until very hot. *Take care in the next step, as the crabs hold moisture and tend to "spit" when they hit the hot fat.* Add the crabs and pan-fry until they are browned and have a reddish hue, 3 to 4 minutes per side. Using tongs, transfer the crabs to paper towels or brown paper bags to drain. (Draining on bags will give you a crisper crust.)

4. To serve, place 2 crabs on each of 2 dinner plates and top with the corn sauce. Serve immediately with the lemon wedges.

THAI Pan-FRIED SOFT-SHELL CRABS

This is a quick sort-of stir-fry with a mild Thai seasoning. The sort-of part is that the crabs cook on one side, then the other, rather than by quick stirring. However, everything moves at a stir-fry pace, so have all your ingredients together and ready to go. Fish sauce is the primary seasoning in Southeast Asian cooking. It is available in the Asian foods section of most large supermarkets. Thai bird chiles are small, very hot peppers that are found in Asian markets and some large supermarkets. **SERVES 2**

1. Combine the fish sauce, honey, chiles, lime juice, and sesame oil in a small bowl. Set aside.

2. Season the crabs with salt and pepper. Place the flour in a pie plate, then dredge the crabs with the flour, tapping off any excess.

3. Melt the butter in a large skillet over medium heat. *Take care in the next step, as the crabs hold moisture and tend to "spit" when they hit the hot butter.* When the butter stops foaming, place the crabs back side down in the pan. Cook for about 2 minutes, turn, and cook for 2 minutes more. Transfer to a platter, cover with aluminum foil, and keep warm.

4. Stir the ginger and garlic into the butter left in the pan and cook until the garlic is fragrant, no more than 1 minute. Pour in the fish sauce mixture and cook, scraping up the browned bits from the bottom of the pan. Cook for about 1 minute. Stir in the cilantro and season with salt and pepper.

5. To serve, place 2 crabs on each of 2 serving plates and spoon the sauce over them. Serve immediately.

1 tablespoon fish sauce

1 teaspoon honey

2 Thai bird chiles or 1 jalapeño, seeded and thinly sliced

¼ cup fresh lime juice

½ teaspoon toasted sesame oil

4 hotel or prime soft-shell crabs, dressed (see page 30)

Kosher salt and freshly ground black pepper to taste

1 cup all-purpose flour

¼ cup (½ stick) unsalted butter

1 teaspoon peeled and finely minced fresh ginger

1 teaspoon minced garlic

¼ cup chopped fresh cilantro leaves

SOFT-SHELL crabs WITH warm bacon and tomato vinaigrette

4 hotel or prime soft-shell crabs, dressed (see page 30)

2 cups buttermilk

1 teaspoon Chesapeake Bay seasoning

Peanut or canola oil for frying

1 cup all-purpose flour

1 cup bottled bacon-spinach salad dressing (the kind sold in the refrigerator section)

2 large ripe tomatoes, peeled, seeded, and diced

4 cups mixed baby greens

This recipe happened totally in spite of myself. Somewhere I read that marinating soft shells in milk gives them a superior taste. I decided buttermilk would be even better. The vinaigrette was a desperate attempt to show off, and it just happens to work. This is my family's favorite soft-shell dish. **SERVES 4**

1. Place the crabs in a glass baking dish large enough to hold them in a single layer. In a measuring cup, combine the buttermilk and Bay seasoning and pour evenly over the crabs. Let sit at room temperature for about 30 minutes.

2. Heat ½ inch of oil in a large skillet over medium-high heat until it shimmers but hasn't started to smoke, about 375°F. Place the flour in a pie plate. Drain the crabs well and dredge them with the flour, tapping off any excess. *Take care in the next step, as the crabs hold moisture and tend to "spit" when they hit the hot fat.* Place several crabs back side down in the oil, being careful not to crowd them, and cook until golden brown, about 2 minutes per side. Using tongs, transfer the crabs to paper towels or brown paper bags to drain. (Draining on bags will give you a crisper crust.)

3. Meanwhile, heat the dressing (a microwave works fine) until hot. Stir in the tomatoes.

4. To serve, divide the greens among 4 serving plates. Top each mound of greens with a crab. Pour the warm dressing over the crabs and dig in.

SOFT-SHELL CRAB CLUB SANDWICH

¼ cup all-purpose flour

½ cup yellow cornmeal, stone-ground preferred

1 teaspoon Chesapeake Bay seasoning

2 large eggs, lightly beaten

1 tablespoon water

Canola or peanut oil for frying

4 hotel or prime soft-shell crabs, dressed (see page 30)

¼ cup mayonnaise

8 slices white or whole wheat sandwich bread

8 strips thick-cut hickory-smoked bacon, cooked until very crisp and drained on paper towels

4 thick ripe tomato slices

8 ripe but firm Hass avocado slices

Romaine lettuce leaves, torn

a fried soft-shell crab placed between 2 pieces of soft white Wonder bread slathered with mayonnaise is really hard to top. But then, every now and again, you just need to step out. This sandwich is "putting on the Ritz." **SERVES 4**

1. Mix together the flour, cornmeal, and Bay seasoning in a pie plate.

2. Combine the eggs and water in another pie plate.

3. Heat ½ inch of oil in a large skillet over medium-high heat until a little cornmeal sprinkled in the pan sizzles as soon as it hits the oil.

4. Meanwhile, dip each crab into the egg mixture, then dredge with the cornmeal mixture. (Use one hand for the wet stuff and one for the dry.) Gently shake any excess cornmeal mixture off the crabs. *Take care in the next step, as the crabs hold moisture and tend to "spit" when they hit the hot oil.* Ease 2 crabs into the oil and fry until golden brown and crispy, about 3 to 4 minutes per side. Using tongs, transfer the crabs to paper towels or brown paper bags to drain. (Draining on bags will give you a crisper crust.) Repeat with the 2 remaining crabs.

5. Make the sandwiches by spreading ½ tablespoon of the mayonnaise on one side of each slice of bread. Place a crab on 4 of the slices. Top each with 2 strips of bacon, a slice of tomato, 2 slices of avocado, and some lettuce. Top with another slice of bread and chow down.

SOFT-SHELL CraBS in SPICY peanut sauce

Soft-shell crabs love being bathed in Southeast Asian flavors. The peanut essence here coaxes another level of sweetness from the crabs. **SERVES 4**

1. In a glass baking dish, soak the crabs in the seasoned milk for 30 minutes at room temperature. Remove from the milk and dredge with the seasoned flour, coating them completely and tapping off any excess.

2. Heat the butter and oil in a large skillet over high heat. *Take care in the next step, as the crabs hold moisture and tend to "spit" when they hit the hot fat.* When the butter stops foaming, place the crabs back side down in the pan. Reduce the heat to medium-high and cook until they are browned and have a reddish hue, about 3 minutes. Carefully turn the crabs and cook for 3 minutes more. Using tongs, transfer the crabs to paper towels or brown paper bags to drain. (Draining on bags will give you a crisper crust.) Place 2 crabs on each of 4 dinner plates.

3. Add the lime juice and wine to the skillet, scraping it to get up the browned bits from the bottom. Stir in the peanut sauce and remove from the heat. Taste and adjust the seasoning with salt, pepper, and Tabasco sauce. Spoon the sauce over the crabs, sprinkle with the cilantro, and serve immediately.

8 hotel or prime soft-shell crabs, dressed (see page 30)

1 cup milk mixed with a dash of Tabasco sauce

1 cup all-purpose flour, lightly seasoned with kosher salt and freshly ground black pepper

2 tablespoons unsalted butter

2 tablespoons canola oil

Juice of 2 limes

½ cup dry white wine

1 tablespoon bottled satay peanut sauce

2 tablespoons chopped fresh cilantro leaves

Grilled Soft-Shell Crabs with Ginger-Lime Sauce

½ cup (1 stick) unsalted butter

Grated zest and juice of 1 lime

1 medium-size shallot, finely chopped

2 teaspoons peeled and finely minced fresh ginger

Kosher salt to taste (optional)

12 hotel or prime soft-shell crabs, dressed (see page 30)

Grilling soft shells has become the "new" method of choice for preparing these seasonal goodies in many of the country's top restaurants. Grilling does take the spatter factor out of your kitchen. The main caveat when grilling soft shells is that they must be basted with a sauce throughout the cooking process to keep them from drying out. This ginger-lime sauce perfumes the crabs with a delicate yet interesting flavor while keeping the critters moist. **SERVES 6**

1. Prepare a medium-hot charcoal fire or preheat a gas grill for medium heat. Set the grate 5 to 6 inches above the heat source.

2. Melt the butter in a small saucepan over medium-low heat. Stir in the lime zest and juice, shallot, and ginger. Taste and add salt, if desired. Keep the sauce warm while the crabs are grilling.

3. Brush each crab with sauce and grill for 5 to 7 minutes per side, depending on their thickness. Brush with the sauce every minute or so to keep the crabs moist. The crabs are done when they turn a reddish brown color and the back feeler legs are crisp.

4. Place the crabs on a heated serving platter, pour the remaining sauce over them, and serve immediately.

Variations: Loads of different flavors can work for your sauce. Add canola oil to your favorite barbecue sauce. Or melt ½ cup (1 stick) unsalted butter and add the juice of 1 lemon, 2 tablespoons chopped fresh Italian parsley leaves, and 1 teaspoon Chesapeake Bay seasoning. Just make sure you have some sort of fat in the sauce.

smoked soft-shell crabs

We smoke everything else, why not soft shells? I like the mild smoke from apple wood to permeate these crabs, but cherry, pecan, and even grapevine cuttings are nice. These crabs are a bit different but really yummy. **SERVES 4**

1. Place the wood chips in a bowl, add water to cover by 1 inch, and set aside to soak for at least 30 minutes. Start a grill that has a cover.

2. Melt the butter in a large nonstick skillet. Add the garlic, basil, cayenne, and ¼ cup of the vermouth. Add the crabs and cook over medium-high heat for 1 minute per side. Transfer the crabs to a flat grilling basket or a mesh grate that has been sprayed or brushed with vegetable oil. Do not discard the contents of the skillet. Drain the apple wood chips and place them over the hot coals. Place the crabs upside down on the grill. Cover the grill and hot-smoke the crabs for 4 to 5 minutes. Turn the crabs over and smoke them for 4 to 5 minutes more. The legs and claws should become partially charred.

3. Transfer the crabs to a serving platter, sprinkle with salt and pepper, and cover to keep warm.

4. Reheat the skillet and add the remaining ¼ cup vermouth, stirring over medium heat for about 30 seconds. Spoon the sauce over the crabs and serve immediately with the lemon wedges.

1 cup apple wood chips

1 tablespoon unsalted butter

2 teaspoons minced garlic

2 tablespoons finely chopped fresh basil leaves or 2 teaspoons dried

⅛ teaspoon cayenne pepper

½ cup dry vermouth

4 hotel or prime soft-shell crabs, dressed (see page 30)

Kosher salt and freshly ground black pepper to taste

½ lemon, cut into 4 wedges

Brunch, Luncheon, and Light Dinner Fare

This may be my favorite chapter. I like to combine several of these recipes into one meal of "little plates," experimenting with multiple flavors and textures. Although pristine freshness of the crab is key to all these dishes, the type of crabmeat you use is very much up to you. Most of these recipes do not need the biggest lump grade and work well with special or claw meat. With the napoleon and tarragon crab pasta, a larger lump is nice.

Crabmeat plays well with many flavors. Spicy Southwestern seasonings and ingredients are particularly good foils for the sweetness of crab. Crab and cheese combine for ultra-rich decadence. Crab and eggs pair well because of the inherent richness of both. Tomatoes love the balance that crabmeat provides. And pasta can help you stretch a pound of crabmeat just a little further. Think of these recipes when you want to throw something special together after a day of outdoor activities or to treat yourself after a hectic and troublesome day.

FISHERMANS WHARF
OF SAN FRANCISCO

Ole's
CRAB SHACK

scrambled eggs with crab, cream cheese, and chives

2 tablespoons sour cream

4 ounces cream cheese, cubed

2 tablespoons unsalted butter

8 large eggs

½ pound crabmeat, lump preferred, picked over for shells and cartilage

2 tablespoons chopped fresh chives

Kosher salt and freshly ground black pepper to taste

2 tablespoons slivered almonds, toasted (see below)

I used this combination of ingredients to make omelets for many years. I liked to make individual omelets, which meant that everybody got served at a different time. But when I tried making a large omelet, everything got messed up. So I started scrambling eggs with the same add-ins, and the taste was just as good. The trick to great scrambled eggs is to beat them, incorporating some air into them, right before they go into the pan, then to drag the eggs from the outside of the pan to the middle, slowly. It's also important not to overcook them. **SERVES 4**

1. Combine the sour cream and cream cheese in a small bowl, mixing until smooth.

2. Melt the butter in a large nonstick skillet over medium heat. While the butter melts, beat the eggs rapidly with a fork. When the butter stops foaming, pour the eggs into the pan. Let them set for a minute, then drag them slowly from the outside of the pan to the middle, spreading them out and dragging them again. Add the cheese mixture, crabmeat, and chives. Continue the drag-and-spread motion until the eggs are just set. Season with salt and pepper and remove from the heat.

3. Serve immediately, sprinkling each serving with almonds.

toasting almonds or any nut

I like to toast small quantities of nuts in a skillet on the stovetop. A nonstick pan works great for this. Heat the pan over medium heat until hot, add the nuts, and shake them around in the pan. Your eyes and nose are the best judges for knowing when they are done. Look for the nuts to take on some color (in the case of pecans, the color gets richer) and wait for a pleasant nutty smell. When the two come together, remove the pan from the heat and pour the nuts onto a plate to prevent further cooking.

easy crab benedict

eggs Benedict in its usual form is a sinfully rich brunch dish. Only one thing could make it better—crabmeat. Gertrude's in Baltimore delights diners with a crab Benedict in which a crab cake replaces the bacon and some Chesapeake Bay seasoning goes into the hollandaise sauce. If you like, you can pan-fry a soft-shell crab instead and put it in the middle of all this glory. I like to use jumbo lump, Dungeness leg, or peekytoe crabmeat.

SERVES 4 NORMAL FOLKS OR 2 VERY HUNGRY ONES

1. To make the sauce, place the egg yolks, Bay seasoning, hot pepper sauce, Worcestershire, and lemon juice in a blender and process until smooth. With the motor running, slowly pour the melted butter into the blender until a thick sauce forms. Season with salt. If necessary, thin with hot water. Pour into a warmed pitcher and keep warm until ready to use.

2. To make the eggs, preheat the oven to 250°F. Place the English muffins cut side up on a baking sheet. Divide the crabmeat among them and put in the oven while you cook the eggs.

3. Fill a 2- to 3-inch-deep sauté pan two-thirds full of water. Add the vinegar and bring to a boil. Break each egg into a shallow coffee cup, then dump the eggs into the water. Reduce the heat to a simmer. With a spoon, shape the eggs, even pour a little water over the top of each one. Cook for 3 to 4 minutes. Part of the beauty of this dish is to have the egg yolks runny.

4. Remove the English muffins from the oven. Remove the eggs with a slotted spoon and drain well. Place 1 egg on each muffin half and plate the muffins. Pour some hollandaise sauce on top and serve immediately.

Blender hollandaise sauce:

8 very fresh large egg yolks (see Note on page 108)

½ teaspoon Chesapeake Bay or Creole seasoning

¼ teaspoon hot pepper sauce

¼ teaspoon Worcestershire sauce

Juice of 1 lemon

1 cup (2 sticks) unsalted butter, melted and kept warm

Kosher salt to taste

Eggs:

2 English muffins, fork split and toasted

1 pound crabmeat, lump preferred, picked over for shells and cartilage

2 tablespoons distilled white vinegar

4 extra-large eggs

a crabby englishman

1 pound crabmeat, picked over for shells and cartilage

¼ cup mayonnaise

1 tablespoon sweet pickle relish

1 teaspoon fresh lemon juice

Kosher salt and freshly ground black pepper to taste

4 English muffins, fork split and toasted

8 slices good-quality Swiss cheese (such as Gruyère or Comté)

8 slices Havarti cheese

The Watermen's Inn is a cozy restaurant in Crisfield, Maryland, that is slightly more upscale than the basic crab shacks found in the city. (I also like the fact that the locals frequent the place.) On its lunch menu is the Crabby Englishman, which is a nice play on words for a crab melt. Crab salad is piled on an English muffin, topped with cheese, and broiled. Crab melts are fairly common among the feeding establishments on the Eastern Shore, and this one is superior. Why? Care is taken with the salad and the quality of the cheese. When questioned, my waitress gave me the basics and I filled in the blanks. This is not the exact recipe from the Watermen's Inn, but it's just as delicious. Use it for a luncheon or late-night supper. Better yet, serve it with champagne on New Year's Eve. **SERVES 4**

1. Preheat the broiler.

2. Combine the crabmeat, mayonnaise, relish, and lemon juice in a medium-size mixing bowl. Season with salt and pepper and toss together.

3. Place the English muffin halves on a baking sheet. Divide the crab salad equally among the muffins. Top each with a slice of Swiss and a slice of Havarti. Broil until the cheese has melted and is beginning to brown, about 5 minutes. Serve as fast as you can.

Variation: Any of the crab salad recipes in this book can be used in this recipe, so if you have found a favorite, feel free to substitute. The same goes for the cheeses. Cheddar or provolone might suit your taste better.

crab quesadillas

Quesadillas have become the finger sandwiches of the new cocktail circuit. They are easy to make if you follow the old French cooking demand of *mise en place*, roughly translated as "everything in its place." By assembling all the ingredients in advance at the stove, this dish becomes as simple as 1-2-3. **MAKES 16 WEDGES; SERVES 6 TO 8**

1. Have all the ingredients except the sour cream and salsa next to the stove.

2. Heat about 2 teaspoons oil in a large nonstick skillet over medium-high heat. Add 1 tortilla and sprinkle with half the cheese, crabmeat, chiles, cilantro, and scallions. Top with another tortilla and press down lightly with a metal spatula. Cook until the tortilla is nicely browned on the bottom and the cheese is starting to melt, 3 to 4 minutes. Carefully turn with the spatula and cook until the other side is nicely browned and the cheese is thoroughly melted. Transfer to a plate. Repeat with the remaining tortillas and filling ingredients.

3. Cut each quesadilla into 8 wedges and serve hot, with bowls of sour cream and salsa on the side.

Vegetable oil for frying

Four 10-inch flour tortillas

6 ounces pepper Jack cheese, shredded

½ pound crabmeat, picked over for shells and cartilage

One 4-ounce can diced mild green chiles, drained

3 tablespoons minced fresh cilantro leaves

3 scallions (white and some of the green part), chopped

Sour cream

Salsa

crab and tomato napoleon

⅓ cup sour cream

1 tablespoon mayonnaise

¼ cup fresh lemon juice

2 tablespoons chopped fresh
  cilantro leaves

2 tablespoons chopped fresh
  chives

Dash or two of hot pepper sauce

1 pound crabmeat, lump or jumbo
  lump backfin blue or
  Dungeness preferred, picked
  over for shells and cartilage

4 large ripe beefsteak tomatoes,
  peeled and each cut into
  4 slices

Extra virgin olive oil as needed

Balsamic vinegar as needed

Here's a recipe to impress your dinner party guests or just to surprise your family. Buy the very best and freshest crabmeat you can afford and shop for the most flavorful tomatoes of the season. In other words, this is a summer treat. **SERVES 4**

1. Blend the sour cream, mayonnaise, lemon juice, cilantro, chives, and hot pepper sauce together in a medium-size mixing bowl. Carefully fold in the crabmeat. Cover with plastic wrap and refrigerate for about 1 hour.

2. When ready to serve, divide the crab into fourths.

3. On each of 4 serving plates, lay down 1 tomato slice and top with some crab mixture. Repeat the layering with the remaining tomato slices and crab, ending with a tomato slice. Drizzle a little oil and vinegar around each napoleon. Serve immediately.

crab-stuffed potatoes

4 large baking potatoes, baked in a 400°F oven until fork tender, about 1 hour

½ cup (1 stick) unsalted butter

½ cup heavy cream

2 cups crabmeat, picked over for shells and cartilage

1 cup shredded medium-sharp cheddar cheese (4 ounces)

1 tablespoon grated yellow onion

1½ teaspoons kosher salt

Paprika for sprinkling

a twice-baked potato is always a treat. Adding crab to the mixture turns something special into something stupendous. This is a good recipe to experiment with inexpensive varieties of crabmeat, even canned. And even though I've suggested cheddar cheese, don't hesitate to substitute your favorite. **SERVES 4 AS A SIDE DISH OR LIGHT SUPPER**

1. Increase the oven temperature to 425°F.

2. When the potatoes are cool enough to handle, cut a 1-inch-wide strip from the top of each. Carefully scoop out the pulp, leaving the shell intact. In a large mixing bowl, mash the pulp with the butter and cream until smooth. Stir in the crabmeat, cheese, onion, and salt. Spoon evenly back into the shells and place on a baking sheet. Sprinkle with paprika and bake until heated through, about 15 minutes.

a simply rich crab fondue

Fondue has come around again in our circular set of food trends. A good fondue depends on the quality of the ingredients that go into the pot. I suggest that you try a Beaufort cheese for this recipe. Beaufort is a French Gruyère-style cheese that's sturdy and smooth. Add a salad, and you have a perfect simple supper for friends, family, or company. If you want a little more flavor, just add some Chesapeake Bay seasoning or Creole seasoning, ½ teaspoon at a time, until you are pleased with the taste. My favorite addition is dried thyme, about ¼ teaspoon. **SERVES 4 TO 6**

1. Melt the cheeses together in the top of a double boiler over gently simmering water, stirring from time to time. Add the cream, stirring to blend. Add the sherry and season with salt and pepper. (Add any other seasonings of your choice at this time.) Add the crabmeat and stir gently to combine. Heat, stirring occasionally, until hot, 5 to 10 minutes.

2. Transfer to a fondue pot, chafing dish, or small slow cooker and serve with the bread cubes for dipping.

½ pound Gruyère or other similar cheese, shredded

One 8-ounce package cream cheese, cubed

¾ cup heavy cream or half-and-half

¼ cup dry sherry

Kosher salt and freshly ground black pepper to taste

1 pound crabmeat, picked over for shells and cartilage

2 loaves crusty French bread, cut into 1-inch cubes

crab rémoulade with fried green tomatoes

½ cup tarragon vinegar

3 tablespoons mayonnaise

3 tablespoons prepared chili
   sauce (I like Bennetts)

1 tablespoon prepared
   horseradish, drained

1 teaspoon finely minced garlic

½ teaspoon paprika

¼ teaspoon kosher salt

¼ teaspoon cayenne pepper

½ cup finely chopped scallions
   (white and green parts)

2 hard-boiled large eggs, peeled
   and finely chopped

1 pound crabmeat, lump
   preferred, picked over for
   shells and cartilage

Fried Green Tomatoes
   (recipe follows)

This is a shortcut rémoulade made with store-bought mayonnaise. The cold, creamy crab against the hot, crisp green tomatoes is a noteworthy blending of tastes and textures. **SERVES 4 TO 6**

1. Combine the vinegar, mayonnaise, chili sauce, horseradish, garlic, paprika, salt, and cayenne in a large bowl. Add the scallions and hard-boiled eggs and stir to combine. Gently fold in the crabmeat. Cover and refrigerate for at least 3 hours, allowing the flavors to meld.

2. Divide the tomatoes among 4 to 6 plates, then divide the rémoulade equally among the tomatoes, placing it on top.

fried green tomatoes

Fried green tomatoes have left the confines of the South and become fancy restaurant fare all over the country. They are easy to make at home, and their crispness and warmth provide a wonderful contrast to velvety crab. Try these tomatoes as a side dish with other seafood or for a hearty breakfast. They are great with Scrambled Eggs with Crab, Cream Cheese, and Chives (page 154). **SERVES 4 TO 6**

1. Combine the buttermilk and cayenne in a large bowl. Add the tomato slices and gently turn in the buttermilk so they are completely coated. Refrigerate for about 1 hour.

2. In a shallow pan, mix together the cornmeal, flour, salt, black pepper, and oregano.

3. Preheat the oven to 200°F.

4. Using one hand for the dry ingredients and the other hand for the wet ingredients, dredge the buttermilk-coated tomatoes with the cornmeal mixture, coating them evenly and well.

5. Heat 3 tablespoons oil in a large sauté pan or cast-iron skillet over medium-high heat. Fry the tomatoes in batches until crisp and golden, about 3 minutes per side. Drain on paper towels or brown paper bags. (Draining on bags will give you a crisper crust.) Transfer to an ovenproof plate and keep warm in the oven until all the tomatoes are fried. Add more oil to the pan, if necessary, as you fry the remaining tomatoes.

6. Sprinkle the tomatoes with salt, if desired, and serve hot.

2 cups buttermilk

¼ teaspoon cayenne pepper

1½ pounds green tomatoes, cored and sliced 1½ inches thick

1½ cups coarse-ground yellow cornmeal

¾ cup all-purpose flour

1 teaspoon kosher salt

1 teaspoon freshly ground black pepper

½ teaspoon dried oregano

Canola or peanut oil for frying

Grilled crab and caramelized onion pizza

2 tablespoons unsalted butter

2 large onions (Vidalia or other sweet onions are best), thinly sliced

1 teaspoon Chesapeake Bay seasoning, or to taste

Yellow cornmeal for sprinkling

Two 10-ounce packages refrigerated pizza dough

½ pound crabmeat, lump preferred, picked over for shells and cartilage

All-Purpose White Sauce (recipe follows)

2 cups shredded Italian 6-cheese blend

Olive oil for drizzling

¼ cup chopped fresh basil leaves

Chopped garlic (optional)

Grilling pizza is a heck of a lot of fun and perfect for an outdoor party, whether you serve it as an appetizer or the whole meal. When you're going to grill a pizza, treat it as you would a stir-fry—have all your ingredients ready and at hand, as everything goes pretty fast.

SERVES 4 TO 6 AS A MEAL

1. Melt the butter in a large skillet over medium heat. When it stops foaming, add the onions and cook slowly, stirring often, for about 15 minutes. Add the Bay seasoning and continue to cook, stirring, until the onions are nicely caramelized, another 15 minutes or so. Remove from the heat.

2. Preheat your gas grill or light the coals. Coat the cooking grid with non-stick cooking spray. Sprinkle 2 pizza peels or baking sheets with cornmeal.

3. Roll and stretch each pizza dough into a rectangle measuring about 8 × 12 inches. Slide the dough onto the grill; don't worry if the rectangles change shape. Cover the grill and cook until the bottom of each pizza is golden brown and crisp, about 7 minutes. Turn the pizzas over. Working quickly, divide the caramelized onions, then the crabmeat, between them. Pour ⅓ cup of the sauce over each pizza. Divide the cheese between the pizzas and drizzle with oil. Cover and grill until the cheese has melted, 5 to 7 minutes.

4. Transfer to the peels or baking sheets. Sprinkle the basil and garlic (if using) over the pizzas and let sit for a couple of minutes before cutting.

aLL-purpose white sauce

Here's a good white sauce recipe not only for this pizza but for any other recipe where you might need one. The gravy flour gives you a little "lump protection," but all-purpose flour works fine. Use freshly grated nutmeg, if you have it, for a more vibrant taste than ground nutmeg will provide. **MAKES ABOUT 1 CUP**

2 tablespoons unsalted butter

2 tablespoons gravy flour (such as Wondra) or all-purpose flour

¾ cup half-and-half

2 teaspoons dry sherry

Pinch of freshly grated nutmeg

Kosher salt and freshly ground black pepper to taste

Melt the butter in a medium-size saucepan over medium heat. When it stops foaming, stir in the flour and cook, stirring, for 2 minutes. Gradually whisk in the half-and-half. Cook, continuing to whisk, until thickened. Stir in the sherry and nutmeg and season with salt and pepper.

a crab roll maine style

Up in Wiscasset, Maine, hiding under a shade tree, is Red's Eats. This tiny place is one of many seafood shacks along the roads of Maine offering simple yet superb food. The crab roll at Red's is classic Maine. Start by adding as little mayonnaise to a pound of picked crab as you can, just to moisten it, probably not more than ¼ cup. Now take a "top-load" (splits on the top) hot dog bun, slather the outside with melted butter, and cook it on a hot griddle or skillet until golden brown and a little crisp. Red's puts a piece of lettuce in the bun, which I think is a total waste of time, then piles in as much of the crab mixture as the bun will hold. The cold crab and the warm bun are heaven on earth.

crab and swiss quiche

½ cup mayonnaise

2 tablespoons all-purpose flour

4 large eggs, lightly beaten

½ cup milk

½ pound crabmeat, lump preferred, picked over for shells and cartilage

½ pound Swiss cheese, shredded

⅓ cup chopped scallions (white and green parts)

1 unbaked 9-inch pie shell

This simple and easy-to-make quiche fills the bill for lunch, brunch, or a late-night supper. Crab marries with eggs in a truly remarkable way. Any variety of crab settles right into this recipe, which even "real men" will enjoy. **MAKES ONE 9-INCH QUICHE; SERVES 4 TO 6**

1. Preheat the oven to 350°F.

2. In a medium-size mixing bowl, thoroughly combine the mayonnaise, flour, eggs, and milk. Gently stir in the crabmeat, cheese, and scallions. Spoon into the pie shell, smoothing the top with a rubber spatula.

3. Bake until firm in the center, 50 to 60 minutes.

4. Let cool on a wire rack for 15 minutes before serving hot, warm, at room temperature, or even cold.

crab "gravy"

a takeoff on country sausage gravy or even creamed chipped beef, this crab gravy beats them both. Crab gravy over toast is fairly common in East Coast crabbing country, but you should also try it over biscuits or rice. This recipe was a way to stretch a pound of crab, but it's pretty chunky and crabby. Add a little more sherry, if you like, for a richer, more regal gravy. This recipe also is superb made with Dungeness crab. **SERVES 4 TO 6**

Melt the butter in a medium-size saucepan over medium-high heat. When it stops foaming, whisk in the flour and cook for about 2 minutes. Add the half-and-half, whisking constantly until thickened. Add the sherry and Bay seasoning, stirring to incorporate. Gently stir in the crab-meat and cook until warm, no more than 5 minutes. Serve hot over toast, biscuits, or rice.

½ cup (1 stick) unsalted butter

½ cup all-purpose flour

1 quart half-and-half or whole milk

1 teaspoon dry sherry

½ teaspoon Chesapeake Bay seasoning

1 pound crabmeat, lump preferred, picked over for shells and cartilage

Toast, biscuits, or cooked white rice

---

chesapeake bay seasoning

a lthough there are many brands and blends of Bay seasoning available for purchase, making your own is fun. This recipe is a starting point. Make this seasoning once as I've suggested, then play with the spices to develop a taste that's perfect for you. Now keep it a secret. **MAKES ABOUT ¾ CUP**

3 tablespoons paprika	1 tablespoon onion powder
2 tablespoons kosher salt	1 tablespoon cayenne pepper
1 to 2 tablespoons garlic powder, to your taste	1 tablespoon dried oregano
1 teaspoon freshly ground black pepper	1 tablespoon dried thyme

Mix everything together and store in an airtight container. Kept in the refrigerator, the seasoning with last for a few months. Shake well before using.

CHEF'S TOPSAIL ISLAND TARRAGON CRAB PASTA

Great chefs fascinate me with their thought processes for complex restaurant creations, but what really blows me away is when they cook for themselves. Great ingredients are transformed into a concert of flavors, each with its solo but also blending in to become part of the whole. When Ben Barker, chef/owner of the Magnolia Grill in Durham, North Carolina, gave me this recipe, his enthusiasm and the sparkle in his eyes told me it was a winner. "Tarragon, with its anise flavor, against crab, how perfect is that?" he asked. He was absolutely right. This recipe is a perfect fit for a week at the beach—few ingredients, little cooking, maximum flavor. I can see Ben now, at his place on Topsail Island, North Carolina, tossing this dish together. **SERVES 4 TO 6**

4 cups ripe cherry or grape tomatoes, halved

3 tablespoons tarragon vinegar

3 tablespoons fresh lemon juice

½ cup olive oil

¼ cup chopped fresh basil leaves

12 ounces bow-tie pasta, cooked until *al dente* and drained

½ pound crabmeat, jumbo lump backfin preferred, picked over for shells and cartilage

Combine the tomatoes, vinegar, lemon juice, olive oil, and basil in a large serving bowl. Add the pasta and toss to coat. Gently fold in the crabmeat. Refrigerate for at least 1 hour or up to 4 hours to let the flavors mingle before serving.

tuscan crab spaghetti

3 tablespoons olive oil

½ cup chopped yellow onion

¼ cup diced celery

¼ cup diced carrots

3 large cloves garlic, roughly chopped

2 tablespoons chopped fresh Italian parsley leaves

One 14.5-ounce can diced tomatoes, undrained

One 8-ounce can tomato sauce

1 teaspoon dried oregano

Freshly ground black pepper to taste

1 pound crabmeat, claw meat or special preferred, picked over for shells and cartilage

1 pound spaghetti, cooked until *al dente* and drained

Freshly grated Parmesan cheese, Parmigiano-Reggiano preferred

This is a recipe that the kids will love and you can make virtually all year round with the different crabmeats as they come into season. Even very well drained canned crabmeat is acceptable, as long as you rinse it to remove excess salt. The carrots give the sauce a natural sweetness that enhances the crab and richens the experience. You can also use the sauce as a basis for crabmeat lasagna. **SERVES 6**

1. Heat the oil in a large skillet over medium heat. Add the onion, celery, and carrots and cook, stirring, until softened, 4 to 5 minutes. Add the garlic and parsley and cook for 1 minute. Pour in the tomatoes and tomato sauce, increase the heat to medium-high, and bring to a boil. Add the oregano and season with pepper. Reduce the heat to a simmer and cook, stirring occasionally, until slightly thickened, 20 to 25 minutes.

2. Add the crabmeat and cook for no more than 5 minutes to heat through.

3. Put the hot cooked pasta in a serving bowl, add the crabmeat sauce, and toss to combine. Pass the cheese at the table.

summer crab pasta

When the blue crabs are fat with pearly white meat, the tomatoes come straight from the garden, and you need a simple, fast, fresh-tasting dinner, reach for this perfect midsummer recipe. Use any pasta that suits your fancy. I like penne because it's easy to eat and the sauce clings to it nicely. **SERVES 4**

1. Heat the oil in a large skillet over medium heat. Add the shallots and cook, stirring, until softened, about 5 minutes. Add the garlic and red pepper flakes and cook until you can smell the garlic, about 1 minute. Add the tomatoes and cook, stirring a few times, for 5 minutes. Add the clam juice and water, bring to a boil, reduce the heat to medium-low, and simmer until slightly thickened, 8 to 10 minutes. Stir in the crabmeat and cook for no more than 5 minutes to heat through. Season with salt and pepper.

2. Place the hot cooked pasta in a serving bowl, add the sauce, and toss well to coat. Sprinkle with the chives and serve immediately.

2 tablespoons fruity extra virgin olive oil

3 large shallots, finely chopped

1 clove garlic, minced

¼ teaspoon red pepper flakes

4 ripe plum or beefsteak tomatoes, seeded and chopped (about 1 cup)

½ cup bottled clam juice

½ cup water

1 pound crabmeat, lump preferred, picked over for shells and cartilage

Kosher salt and freshly ground black pepper to taste

1 pound penne, cooked until *al dente* and drained

¼ cup chopped fresh chives

casseroles, easy sautés, and one incredible indulgence

To enter this chapter, you need to check your fears of butter and cream at the door, because rich ingredients and crab have a natural affinity for one another. Many of the classic and traditional crab recipes are casseroles and quick sautés. Crab Norfolk is one of my favorites. It takes just minutes to prepare, yet tastes as if it required all grades of trouble to get to the table. Many folks in the Chesapeake Bay area will quickly tell you that after steamed crabs, they enjoy a good crab casserole over all other dishes, even crab cakes. All of these recipes are rich and decadent. Folks swoon over a great crab imperial or a properly prepared deviled crab. These concoctions are wonderful for entertaining. Most can be made ahead, even frozen, and popped in the oven when the guests arrive.

crab imperial

3 tablespoons unsalted butter

2 tablespoons finely chopped
yellow onion

1 tablespoon seeded and finely
chopped green bell pepper

2 tablespoons all-purpose flour

½ cup milk or heavy cream

1 tablespoon dry sherry

2 tablespoons mayonnaise

½ teaspoon Chesapeake Bay
seasoning

¼ teaspoon freshly ground black
pepper

¼ teaspoon Worcestershire
sauce

1 pound crabmeat, lump
preferred, picked over for
shells and cartilage

Paprika for sprinkling

I guess I was a little shocked when I discovered that *The Joy of Cooking* did not have a recipe for crab imperial. This is a classic American dish. Webster's *New World Dictionary of Culinary Arts* defines crab imperial as "a dish of crabmeat bound with mayonnaise or a sherried cream sauce and placed in blue crab shells, sprinkled with bread crumbs or Parmesan cheese and baked." *The Food Lover's Companion* describes it similarly. What I've found out about crab imperial is that the recipes for it are closely guarded family secrets that are passed from generation to generation and that it can make or break a restaurant in the Chesapeake Bay region. Of course, if you eat enough crab imperial and pester people long enough, you can get a decent idea of how it is made. This is my interpretation of all the bits and pieces of recipes I have culled from scores of folks on the bay. It's a great place to start. **SERVES 6**

1. Preheat the oven to 350°F. Grease a 2-quart baking dish or 6 individual ramekins, if preferred.

2. Melt the butter in a large skillet over medium heat. When it stops foaming, add the onion and bell pepper and cook, stirring, until softened, about 5 minutes. Stir in the flour, then pour in the milk, stirring. Cook, stirring, until thickened, 2 to 3 minutes. Remove from the heat.

3. In a medium-size mixing bowl, combine the sherry, mayonnaise, Bay seasoning, black pepper, and Worcestershire. Gently fold in the crabmeat. Pour the sauce over the mixture and gently combine. Spoon into the prepared baking dish or ramekins or into cleaned crab shells (see page 176). Sprinkle with paprika. Bake until bubbling, 20 to 25 minutes. Serve hot.

crab imperial baltimore style

Some crab imperial recipes break from the usual white sauce and use mayonnaise to hold everything together. I found more of that style around Baltimore and Annapolis, Maryland, and along the western shore of the Chesapeake Bay. It's just as delightful and a little easier to prepare than the classic presentation. Although you can use white mushrooms in this recipe, brown or wild mushrooms will lend a pleasant earthiness to the dish. **SERVES 4**

1. Preheat the oven to 350°F.

2. Melt the butter in a small skillet over medium heat. When it stops foaming, add the bell pepper and mushrooms and cook, stirring, until softened, about 5 minutes. Remove from the heat.

3. In a medium-size mixing bowl, blend together the mayonnaise, mustard, Worcestershire, scallions, hot pepper sauce, black pepper and Bay seasoning. Stir in the sautéed peppers and mushrooms. Gently fold in the crabmeat. Spoon the mixture into an ungreased 9 × 13-inch baking dish, 4 individual gratin dishes, or 4 cleaned crab shells (see page 176). Place on a baking sheet and bake until bubbling, 20 to 25 minutes. You can prepare the dish up to this point an hour or so before serving.

4. Meanwhile, make the topping. Combine all the ingredients in a small bowl.

5. When ready to serve, preheat the broiler.

6. Spoon the topping over the casserole or each serving. Broil until nicely browned, 1 to 2 minutes. Serve immediately.

¼ cup (½ stick) unsalted butter

3 tablespoons seeded and diced green bell pepper

½ cup finely chopped white, brown, or wild mushrooms

¾ cup mayonnaise

1 tablespoon Creole or other grainy mustard

1 tablespoon Worcestershire sauce

1 tablespoon chopped scallions (white and green parts)

Dash of hot pepper sauce

½ teaspoon freshly ground black pepper

1 teaspoon Chesapeake Bay seasoning, or more to taste

1 pound crabmeat, lump preferred, picked over for shells and cartilage

Topping:

1 large egg, lightly beaten

⅓ cup mayonnaise

1 tablespoon mixed chopped fresh herbs, such as Italian parsley and tarragon leaves

¼ teaspoon paprika

country ham and crab imperial

1 large egg, lightly beaten

¾ cup mayonnaise

½ cup sour cream

1 teaspoon dry mustard

1 teaspoon Chesapeake Bay
seasoning

½ teaspoon dried thyme

1 tablespoon chopped fresh
Italian parsley leaves

1 pound crabmeat, jumbo lump
backfin preferred, picked over
for shells and cartilage

8 paper-thin slices country ham
or prosciutto

¼ cup (½ stick) unsalted butter,
melted

Lemon wedges

Crab and cured country ham have long been a favorite pairing, and nowhere is that affinity realized better than in crab imperial. This recipe was inspired by many recipes I found in community cookbooks from the tidewater area of Virginia. Country hams are cured differently through-out the South and Midwest. This dish is excellent with prosciutto or speck ham. Pick your ham and crabmeat of choice and make this dish all your own. For an over-the-top breakfast, serve this with scrambled eggs and biscuits.

SERVES 4

1. Preheat the oven to 400°F. Butter 4 individual baking dishes or a 2-quart casserole.

2. Combine the egg, mayonnaise, sour cream, dry mustard, Bay seasoning, thyme, and parsley in a medium-size mixing bowl. Gently fold in the crabmeat.

3. Place 2 pieces of the ham in each baking dish, or place all 8 pieces in the casserole. Spread the crab mixture over the ham, then drizzle the melted butter on top. Bake until golden brown, about 15 minutes. Serve at once with lemon wedges.

---

prepping crab shells for serving

Select large, unbroken shells. Using a brush, scrub them in warm water until clean. Place in a large pot with 1 teaspoon baking soda and water to cover. Bring to a boil, reduce the heat to medium-low, and simmer for 20 minutes. Drain. Wash again and dry. Now the shells are ready to use for deviled crab, crab imperial, or other casseroles. When baking in a crab shell, reduce the cooking time suggested in the recipe by 5 minutes and look for a golden brown top.

classic deviled crab

If your first thought after the words "deviled crab" is the plate filler used on seafood platters, you are in for a treat. To devil is to add a few hot and spicy ingredients to a dish, and most of those platter fillers are deviling bread crumbs more than they are crab. Along the East Coast in the 1920s, deviling was the culinary equal to comfort foods today—the hip trend. Historically, deviled crab has been served in the top shell of the crab, but it is easy to prepare in a casserole or individual baking dishes. You may find the use of hard-boiled eggs strange, but it is authentic. **SERVES 4 TO 6**

1. Preheat the oven to 375°F. Butter a 1½-quart casserole.

2. Melt the butter in a medium-size skillet over medium heat. When it stops foaming, add the onion and cook, stirring, until softened, 2 to 3 minutes. Add the flour and dry mustard and whisk until blended. Whisk in the milk, Creole mustard, Worcestershire, hot pepper sauce, salt, black pepper, and cayenne and cook, stirring, until thickened, about 8 minutes. Remove from the heat and let cool slightly.

3. In a medium-size mixing bowl, gently fold together the eggs, crabmeat, parsley, and lemon juice. Pour the mustard sauce over the mixture and fold to combine. Scrape into the prepared casserole and sprinkle evenly with the crackers. Bake until golden brown, about 30 minutes. Serve hot.

¼ cup (½ stick) unsalted butter

2 tablespoons finely chopped yellow onion

2 tablespoons all-purpose flour

1 teaspoon dry mustard

1 cup milk, half-and-half, or heavy cream

1 teaspoon Creole or other grainy mustard

½ teaspoon Worcestershire sauce

¼ teaspoon hot pepper sauce

1 teaspoon kosher salt

¼ teaspoon freshly ground black pepper

⅛ teaspoon cayenne pepper

2 hard-boiled large eggs, peeled and finely chopped

1 pound crabmeat, lump preferred, picked over for shells and cartilage

1 tablespoon chopped fresh Italian parsley leaves

1 teaspoon fresh lemon juice

¾ cup roughly crushed butter crackers (such as Ritz)

crisfield crab casserole

3 tablespoons mayonnaise

3 tablespoons salad dressing (such as Miracle Whip)

1 tablespoon distilled white vinegar

1½ teaspoons prepared yellow or Dijon mustard

2 large eggs, lightly beaten

½ teaspoon Chesapeake Bay seasoning

Dash of Worcestershire sauce

Kosher salt and freshly ground black pepper to taste

1 pound crabmeat, Smith Island Special Deluxe preferred, picked over for shells and cartilage

½ cup corn flake crumbs

2 tablespoons chopped fresh Italian parsley leaves

3 tablespoons unsalted butter, cut into small pieces

Up and down the Eastern Shore, easy-to-make crab casseroles are a tradition for supper on the Wednesday before Thanksgiving. That just might be a tradition you should adopt. This recipe comes by way of Shirley Hoheisel of Crisfield, Maryland, and it's mighty good. **SERVES 4 TO 6**

1. Preheat the oven to 475°F. Butter a 9 × 13-inch casserole.

2. In a medium-size mixing bowl, combine the mayonnaise, salad dressing, vinegar, mustard, eggs, Bay seasoning, Worcestershire, and salt and pepper. Gently fold in the crabmeat until well combined. Scrape into the prepared casserole.

3. In a small mixing bowl, stir together the corn flake crumbs and parsley. Sprinkle evenly over the crab mixture, then dot with the butter. Bake until bubbling, 20 to 25 minutes. Remove from the oven, let cool slightly (about 5 minutes), and serve.

northwest crab
and wild rice bake

Susan Massey, a friend who hails from Oregon, shared this recipe with me. It features the local flavors of the area—wild rice, mushrooms, and Tillamook cheddar—to go along with the Dungeness crab. The result is a casserole worthy of company. And don't you snicker at the condensed soup. Where would casseroles be without it? If you live on the East Coast, blue or Maine crabmeat will work just fine. **SERVES 4 TO 6**

1. Preheat the oven to 350°F.

2. Melt the butter in a medium-size skillet over medium-high heat. When it stops foaming, add the mushrooms and cook, stirring, until the liquid has evaporated, about 5 minutes. Remove from the heat.

3. In a medium-size mixing bowl, combine the soup and half-and-half. Layer an ungreased round 2-quart casserole as follows: half the rice, half the crabmeat, half the soup mixture, and half the mushrooms. Repeat. Cover the top evenly with the cheeses. Cover and bake until bubbly, about 30 minutes. Serve hot.

2 tablespoons unsalted butter

¼ pound white or brown mushrooms, thinly sliced

One 14.75-ounce can condensed cream of mushroom soup

½ cup half-and-half

8 ounces wild rice, cooked according to package directions and drained, if necessary

1 pound crabmeat, Dungeness preferred, picked over for shells and cartilage

½ cup finely shredded Swiss cheese

½ cup finely shredded Tillamook or other sharp cheddar cheese

JIM VILLAS'S SAVANNAH DEVILED CRAB CRUSTED WITH PECANS

1 pound crabmeat, lump preferred, picked over for shells and cartilage

1 large stalk celery, finely chopped

1 medium-size green bell pepper, seeded and finely chopped

4 scallions (white and green parts), finely chopped

¼ cup chopped fresh Italian parsley leaves

½ teaspoon dry mustard

Kosher salt and freshly ground black pepper to taste

Tabasco sauce to taste

¼ cup heavy cream

½ cup (1 stick) unsalted butter, melted

1½ cups roughly crushed soda crackers

½ cup finely chopped pecans

Jim Villas is a first-rate American food writer who has traveled the world and yet remains loyal to his Southern roots. Jim's mother, Martha Pearl Villas, is an excellent cook, and Jim has learned volumes from her. In recent years, they have teamed up to write 3 books on what I call home food with an upscale attitude. This recipe is from Jim's latest book, *Crazy for Casseroles.* I love the Southern bent given to this recipe by the use of pecans as a topping. The rich, sweet taste of the nuts melds perfectly with the crab. But, warns Jim, rancid nuts will destroy this dish. **SERVES 4**

1. Preheat the oven to 350°F. Butter a 1½-quart casserole.

2. In a large mixing bowl, gently combine the crabmeat, celery, bell pepper, scallions, parsley, mustard, and salt and pepper. Add the Tabasco, cream, half the butter, and the crackers and stir gently to combine.

3. Scrape the mixture into the prepared casserole or into cleaned crab shells (see page 176), sprinkle the pecans evenly on top, and drizzle with the remaining butter. Bake until golden brown, about 30 minutes. Serve hot.

kate graves's crab supreme

½ cup water

1 cup diced celery

6 slices white bread

1 cup chopped yellow onion

½ cup seeded and diced green
  bell pepper

½ cup mayonnaise

½ teaspoon kosher salt

1 pound crabmeat, picked over
  for shells and cartilage

4 large eggs, lightly beaten

3 cups whole milk

One 14.75-ounce can condensed
  cream of mushroom soup

1 cup finely shredded cheese (a
  mixture of Swiss, Monterey
  Jack, and Parmesan is good)

Paprika for sprinkling

michael Rider of Richmond, Virginia, loves to cook and has won many blue ribbons for his cakes, preserves, and other goodies at the State Fair of Virginia. Michael also enjoys entertaining and often includes this dish in buffets and luncheons, always drawing rave reviews. Michael acquired this recipe as a teenager working at the Graves Mountain Lodge in Syria, Virginia. Kate Graves was the owner's mother, and her recipe was served at the lodge for many a ladies' luncheon. Keep this as a secret weapon in your entertaining arsenal. **SERVES 10 TO 12**

1. Bring the water to a boil in a small saucepan. Add the celery, reduce the heat to a simmer, and cook for 10 minutes. Drain and set aside.

2. Dice 3 slices of the bread and sprinkle evenly in a greased long, shallow 2-quart casserole.

3. In a medium-size mixing bowl, mix together the onion, bell pepper, mayonnaise, salt, and celery. Gently fold in the crabmeat. Spread this mixture over the diced bread. Dice the remaining 3 slices of bread and sprinkle evenly over the crab mixture. Combine the eggs and milk in a medium-size mixing bowl and pour over the casserole. Cover and refrigerate overnight.

4. Preheat the oven to 325°F.

5. Uncover the casserole and bake for 15 minutes. Remove from the oven and pour the soup over the top. Sprinkle evenly with the cheese and paprika, return to the oven, and continue to bake until golden brown, about 1 hour. Serve hot.

T's crabmeat divan with mornay sauce

My mother, "T," as we lovingly call her, didn't fix many crab dishes when I was growing up. When she did bring crab into the house, it usually was prepared in this fashion. I believe it was her way of getting the family to eat broccoli, and it worked beautifully in this opulent casserole. **SERVES 6**

1. To make the Mornay sauce, melt the butter in a medium-size saucepan over medium heat. When it stops foaming, stir in the flour, then whisk in the milk. Cook, stirring, until the sauce begins to thicken, 3 to 4 minutes. Add the cheeses and Bay seasoning and season with salt and pepper. Stir until well blended, then remove from the heat.

2. Preheat the oven to 350°F.

3. To assemble the casserole, place the broccoli in an ungreased shallow 1½-quart casserole. Cover evenly with the crabmeat. Top with 1 cup of the Mornay sauce, then sprinkle evenly with the bread crumbs. Bake until browned and bubbly, about 25 minutes. Serve hot.

Note: Any leftover Mornay sauce can be refrigerated for 3 to 4 days. It is delicious served over asparagus, used as a white pizza sauce, or spooned over chicken breasts.

Mornay sauce:

2 tablespoons unsalted butter

2 tablespoons all-purpose flour

1 cup whole milk

¼ cup shredded Swiss cheese

¼ cup freshly grated Parmesan cheese

½ teaspoon Chesapeake Bay seasoning

Kosher salt and freshly ground black pepper to taste

Casserole:

1 bunch broccoli (about 1¼ pounds), steamed whole until tender, then stems and florets chopped, or two 10-ounce boxes frozen chopped broccoli, defrosted, drained, and squeezed dry

1 pound crabmeat, lump preferred, picked over for shells and cartilage

¼ cup seasoned dry bread crumbs

crab norfolk

¼ cup (½ stick) unsalted butter

1 pound crabmeat, lump or jumbo lump backfin preferred, picked over for shells and cartilage

2 tablespoons good-quality sherry vinegar (not cooking sherry)

3 dashes of hot pepper sauce

Pinch of kosher salt

1 grind of black pepper

Cooked white rice or frozen puff pastry shells, baked according to the package directions

Variations on this recipe have been around for decades. It's also one of my favorite crab preparations. Simple, quick, yet rich and satisfying, it is the very essence of the sea. History tells us that this dish was created at the Snowden and Mason Restaurant in Norfolk, Virginia, in the 1920s. My first taste of it was actually in the low country of South Carolina and around the Bogue Banks area of North Carolina, where you'll find excellent crab "panned," or sautéed, in butter. This particular recipe, however, came by way of relatives in the Norfolk area. **SERVES 4 TO 6**

1. Melt the butter in a large skillet over medium heat. When it foams, add the crabmeat, vinegar, hot pepper sauce, salt, and black pepper. Carefully, so as not to break up those precious lumps of crab, swirl the pan until the crab is warmed through, 3 to 5 minutes. *Do not overcook.*

2. Serve immediately over rice or spooned into puff pastry shells. For me, a bowl and a spoon work just fine.

down-home crab creole

along the Gulf coast, there are as many versions of crab Creole as there are cooks. All start from the classic base of onion, bell pepper, and celery—what's known in south Louisiana as the holy trinity. This one requires the addition of a little bacon fat for flavoring. After rendering the bacon, consider the crispy strips a cook's treat. **SERVES 4 TO 6**

1. In a large skillet, cook the bacon over medium heat until it is crisp and has rendered its fat. Remove the bacon and save for another use or enjoy it yourself (no one's looking).

2. Add the onion, bell pepper, and celery to the skillet. Increase the heat to medium-high and cook, stirring, until softened, 5 to 6 minutes. Add the garlic and cook for 1 minute. Add the tomatoes, sugar, Worcestershire, hot pepper sauce, and salt and pepper. Reduce the heat to medium and simmer for about 15 minutes.

3. Gently stir in the crabmeat and cook for 5 minutes to heat through. Serve over rice, garnished with the scallions, if desired. Pass more hot pepper sauce at the table.

4 strips thick-cut smoked bacon (apple wood smoked is best)

1 cup chopped onion

½ cup seeded and chopped green bell pepper

½ cup chopped celery

1 teaspoon finely chopped garlic

One 16-ounce can peeled whole tomatoes, undrained

1 teaspoon sugar

1 teaspoon Worcestershire sauce

2 to 3 dashes of hot pepper sauce, to your taste, plus more for serving

Kosher salt and freshly ground black pepper to taste

1 pound crabmeat, lump preferred, picked over for shells and cartilage

Cooked white rice

¼ cup chopped scallions (white and green parts; optional)

curried crab

2 tablespoons canola oil

1 cup diced sweet onion

½ cup seeded and finely diced red bell pepper

2 teaspoons minced garlic

About 1¼ cups canned unsweetened coconut milk (see Note)

One 14.5-ounce can diced tomatoes, undrained

1 large Granny Smith apple, peeled, cored, and finely diced

1 serrano chile or jalapeño, seeded and chopped (leave in the seeds for a hotter dish)

1 tablespoon peeled and chopped fresh ginger

1½ tablespoons good-quality curry powder

⅛ teaspoon ground cinnamon

1 tablespoon sugar

1 tablespoon all-purpose flour

2 tablespoons cold water

1½ pounds crabmeat, backfin preferred, picked over for shells and cartilage

2 tablespoons fresh lime juice

2 tablespoons chopped fresh cilantro leaves, or more to taste

Kosher salt and white pepper to taste

Cooked basmati or other long-grain white rice

Lime wedges

Curry-infused dishes have graced Southern tables for centuries, due in large part to the lively spice trade and the influence of African cooking. Many of these areas had an abundance of blue crabs, so combining the two was only natural. Most of the curries were Indian style, toned down for European and American tastes. This recipe is updated with a more Southeast Asian tone. It's hot and bold, with a fruitiness sure to please. Any variety or style of crabmeat will work well. You can turn up the heat by including the seeds of the chile and increasing the amount of curry powder and ginger.

SERVES 6

1. Heat the oil in a large saucepan over medium-high heat. Add the onion and bell pepper and cook, stirring, until softened, about 5 minutes. Add the garlic and cook until you can smell it, about 1 minute. Pour in 1 cup of the coconut milk and the tomatoes and cook for 2 minutes. Add the apple, chile, and ginger and bring to a boil. Reduce the heat to medium-low, cover, and simmer for 10 minutes.

2. Combine the curry powder, cinnamon, sugar, and flour in a small bowl. Add the water and stir to make a smooth paste. Add to the saucepan, whisking constantly, and bring to a boil. Reduce the heat to medium-low, partially cover, and simmer for 15 to 20 minutes, stirring often. If the curry gets too thick, thin it with more of the coconut milk as needed.

3. Add the crabmeat, lime juice, and cilantro. Stir gently to combine and heat for no longer than 5 minutes. Season with salt and white pepper. Serve with the rice and lime wedges.

Note: Canned unsweetened coconut milk can be found in the Asian foods section of most supermarkets.

crabmeat stuffing

Premade crab stuffing and much of what is served in restaurants just isn't very good. This recipe takes very little time to make and is so much better than store-bought that you'll be stuffing everything in sight. Just cut the recipe in half if you don't need this much. **MAKES ENOUGH STUFFING FOR 8 SINGLE PORTIONS**

Melt the butter in a large skillet over medium heat. When it stops foaming, add the shallots and cook, stirring, for 2 minutes. Stir in the crumbs, crackers, parsley, chives, and lemon juice. Gently fold in the crabmeat, salt, and pepper. Remove from the heat and refrigerate until ready to use.

¼ cup (½ stick) unsalted butter

3 tablespoons finely chopped shallots

1 cup fresh bread crumbs

½ cup roughly crushed butter crackers (such as Ritz)

2 tablespoons chopped fresh Italian parsley leaves

1 tablespoon chopped fresh chives

1 tablespoon fresh lemon juice

1 pound crabmeat, lump preferred, picked over for shells and cartilage

½ teaspoon kosher salt

¼ teaspoon freshly ground black pepper

---

some quick stuffing ideas

For Fish: Flounder and sole fillets are great for stuffing. Cut each fillet lengthwise into 3 strips. Place 1 strip in a buttered baking dish, mound ¼ to ⅓ cup crab stuffing in the middle, and lay the other 2 strips on each side of the stuffing. Bake or broil to your liking. You can also put a mound of stuffing on a single fillet, roll it up, place it in a buttered baking dish, pour 1 to 2 tablespoons sherry in the dish, and bake to your liking.

For Steak: With a boning knife, cut a lengthwise slit in the side of a steak, making a pocket. Put as much stuffing as you can in the pocket. Grill or broil to your desired degree of doneness.

For Chicken: Place boneless, skinless chicken cutlets between plastic wrap and pound to an even thickness. Remove the wrap and place a portion of stuffing in the center of each cutlet. Roll up around the stuffing and place seam side down in a greased baking dish. Pour over one 14.75-ounce can condensed cream of mushroom or cream of asparagus soup and bake in a preheated 350°F oven for 40 minutes.

grilled filets mignons with crab newburg sauce

Crab Newburg sauce:

¼ cup (½ stick) unsalted butter

2 tablespoons chopped yellow
 onion

1½ cups sliced white or brown
 mushrooms

¼ cup all-purpose flour

½ teaspoon kosher salt

½ teaspoon paprika

Freshly ground black pepper to
 taste

1½ cups milk

1 teaspoon Worcestershire sauce

2 large egg yolks, lightly beaten

2 tablespoons dry white wine

¾ pound crabmeat, picked over
 for shells and cartilage

Filets:

Six ½-pound filets mignons

Kosher salt and freshly ground
 black pepper to taste

Olive oil for drizzling

This is truly a celebratory dish—tender grilled filets mignons complemented by an opulent crab sauce. The Newburg sauce is a take-off on lobster Newburg, which is a mixture of cream, butter, eggs, cognac, and black pepper. I think the cognac is a little sharp with the crabmeat, but add some if you wish. Delmonico's restaurant in New York City first popularized lobster Newburg in the 1800s, when Ben Wenberg, a fruit importer and a Delmonico's regular, introduced the chef to a lobster dish he had eaten in his travels. The chef was so impressed with the dish that he named it after Wenberg—Lobster Wenberg. One night, Wenberg got drunk at Delmonico's, started a fight, and was banned from the restaurant. As further punishment, the chef renamed his dish lobster Newburg. Don't pour the sauce over the filets, but around them, so that diners taste the beef and the sauce independently or together, as they choose. **SERVES 6**

1. To make the sauce, melt the butter in a medium-size skillet over medium heat. When the butter stops foaming, add the onion and mushrooms and cook, stirring, until softened, about 5 minutes. Add the flour, salt, paprika, and pepper, stirring to combine. Whisk in the milk and Worcestershire and cook, stirring constantly, until thickened. Remove from the heat and let cool just slightly.

2. Place the egg yolks in a small bowl and beat in ¼ cup of the sauce. Add the mixture back to the sauce, stirring well to combine. Stir in the wine and crabmeat. Transfer to the top of a double boiler set over gently simmering water to keep warm while you grill the filets.

3. Light your coals or preheat your gas grill.

4. Season the filets with salt and pepper. Drizzle a small amount of oil on both sides. When your coals are ash gray or your gas grill is hot, grill the filets, turning once, to your desired degree of doneness, about 15 minutes total for medium. Remove from the grill and let rest for 5 minutes.

5. Serve hot, passing the crab sauce at the table.

crab festivals

If you're interested in attending any of these festivals, I strongly recommend that you call ahead to confirm that the festival is still held and what the dates are for that particular year.

alaska

Kodiak Crab Festival
Late May
(907) 486-5557
www.kodiak.org

california

World Championship Crab Races, Crescent City
Sunday before Presidents' Day
(800) 343-8300

Mendocino Crab & Wine Days
Last weekend in January through first weekend in
   February
(866) 466-3636
www.gomendo.com/events/crab

florida

Blue Crab Festival, Palatka
Always Memorial Day weekend
(386) 325-4406
www.bluecrabfestival.com

Blue Crab Festival, Panacea
First weekend in May
(850) 984-CRAB
www.bluecrab-festival.com

louisiana

Bayou Lacombe Crab Festival
Last week in June
(800) 634-9443 or (985) 892-0520

maryland

National Hard Crab Derby & Fair, Crisfield
Always Labor Day weekend
(800) 782-3913 or (410) 698-2500
www.crisfield.org/crabderby.cfm

new york

Howard Beach Crab Race

(718) 835-0454

north carolina

Blue Crab Festival, Bayboro

Labor Day

(252) 745-3133

oregon

Crab Bounty Hunt, Winchester Bay

August

(800) 247-2155

www.winchesterbay.org/crab.html

south carolina

Blue Crab Festival, Little River

May

(843) 249-4252

texas

Texas Crab Festival, Crystal Beach

Last weekend in April

(409) 684-5940

www.crystalbeach.com/crabfest.htm

virginia

West Point Crab Carnival

First weekend in October

(804) 843-4620

www.westpointva.com/crabcarn

washington

Westport Crab Festival

Third weekend in April

(800) 345-6223

index

PHOTO ACKNOWLEDGMENTS:

Corbis, page 61, lower right; page 153, upper right
Faidley's Seafood, page 95, upper left; page 123, left; page 135, lower left
Greater Newport Chamber of Commerce, Oregon, page 95, upper right; page 191, right
Jodi Marchowsky, page 61, upper right; page 122, right
Mendocino County Alliance with permission from John Birchard, page 61, upper left; page 81, upper right; page 115, lower left; page 135, upper left; page 153, upper left and lower right; page 173, lower left and lower right; page 190, right
Mendocino County Alliance with permission from Caito Fisheries, page 81, lower left; page 115, lower left
OSU Sea Grant/Oregon Dungeness Crab Commission, page 81, upper left and lower right; page 95, lower left; page 115, upper left; page 116, lower left and upper right; page 123, right; page 135, upper left; page 153, lower left; page 190, left
© Greg Pease, with permission from Faidley's Seafood, page 123, left
Photodisc, page 61, lower right; page 153, upper right
Swan Oyster Depot, San Francisco, page 116, upper left
Fred Thompson, all photos on pages 11, 33, 96, and 136; page 61, lower left; page 95, lower right; page 115, upper right and lower right; page 122, left; page 135, lower right; page 173, upper left and upper right; page 191, left

All recipe photography by Brian Hagiwara